Puglia Travel Guide 2024

Discover Puglia: A Journey Through Southern Italy Wonderful Region with an Apulian Native Insider, Following the advice of a local guide and don't miss the incredible.

Rick Paul

Puglia Revealed: A Journey of Connection

It all started with a captivating postcard—a photograph of Puglia's rugged coastline, bathed in the warm glow of the setting sun. That single image ignited a desire for adventure, setting me on a transformative journey to Puglia and planting the seed for a mission to make this remarkable destination accessible to all.

Puglia greeted me with a stunning contrast of landscapes: the serene Adriatic Sea met the vibrant tapestry of this historic region. Olive groves coexisted with contemporary art, and medieval towns shared space with modern beach resorts, creating a unique blend of old and new.

Exploring Puglia led me through the winding streets of Ostuni and the enchanting trulli houses of Alberobello. But it was the warmth of the people that truly captivated me—the farmers who welcomed me into their olive groves, the chefs who shared their culinary secrets, and the artisans who showcased their talents in the cobbled streets of Lecce.

As I pen these words, I extend an invitation to you, dear reader. Join me in discovering the secrets of Puglia, making your journey here as enriching and accessible as possible. Let's experience the hidden treasures, savor the flavors, and connect with the warmth of Puglia, together.

Contents

Italy puglia trani cathedral

An Overview of Puglia

Take a Trip Through Puglia's Enchanting Tapestry

Welcome to a world where sun-kissed coasts meet ancient olive orchards, where the perfume of blooming flowers blends with the aroma of traditional cuisine, and where history, culture, and natural beauty join together to offer an experience unlike any other. Step into the pages of "Puglia Travel Guide" and be transported to a world of eternal beauty and limitless discovery.

Puglia, Southern Italy's crown treasure, entices adventurers, foodies, culture lovers, and wanderers alike. Its surroundings are a work of art in contrasts, with pristine beaches caressing crystal-clear waters, gorgeous cities whispering stories of antiquity, and rolling farmland bearing witness to years of agricultural traditions. As you read through this book, you'll find yourself immersed in a symphony of activities celebrating Puglia's essence.

"Puglia Travel Guide" is your key to unlocking the wonders of this wonderful region, whether you're savoring the rich aromas of locally made olive oil, going back in time amidst the complex architecture, or participating in exciting festivals that pulse with life. Every page is an invitation to discover, taste, learn, and interact with a culture that has existed for ages.

Join us on a journey to hidden coves, lovely trattorias, and the heart of Puglian culture. Allow the guide to be your compass, guiding you to activities that resonate with the very spirit of this lovely destination as the golden sunsets paint the countryside in amber hues.

Embrace the appeal, beauty, and richness that Puglia has to offer, and let "Puglia Travel Guide" accompany you on an extraordinary journey through a world that promises astonishment at every turn. Your journey begins here.

1.1 Hello and welcome to Puglia.

Hello and welcome to Puglia, a fascinating region in southern Italy! Allow me to introduce you to the delights that await you as you embark on your journey through this fascinating region. Puglia, sometimes known as the "heel of Italy's boot," has a unique blend of history, culture, and natural beauty that ensures an unforgettable experience.

Consider exploring a realm where ancient traditions coexist with technology marvels. Puglia is a region where natural beaches along the Salento Peninsula meet with the charm of old towns such as Bari and Lecce. This tour will take you on an adventure to discover the secrets of a nation rich in traditions and shaped by centuries of history.

Prepare to be swept away by Alberobello's beautiful Trulli structures, which, with their distinctive conical roofs, offer a look into the past. Dive into the depths of Grotte di Castellana, a millennia-old natural underground wonderland.

During your travels in Puglia, you will encounter a warm and welcoming local culture. Each meal tells a story about the region's agricultural past and seaside riches, making the culinary scene an experience in and of itself. Enjoy the melt-in-your-mouth sweetness of burrata cheese and the sharpness of locally produced olive oil, both of which have long been a part of Puglian life.

Puglia's towns, villages, and natural landscapes

exhibit a rich tapestry of influences that have shaped the region's identity over time. Every turn reveals a slice of history, from ancient Greek and Roman ruins to stunning Baroque architecture.

Throughout this book, you'll find information to help you organize an unforgettable trip to Puglia. You'll have everything you need to make the most of your vacation, from crucial travel information to insider suggestions on the best times to visit. So immerse yourself in the beauty of Puglia and let this guide be your steadfast companion as you discover the mysteries of this amazing province. Prepare for an extraordinary experience that will leave you with lifelong memories.

1.2 Geography and Climate

Now that you've been warmly welcomed to Puglia, let's have a look at the geographical wonders and climate that set this unique region apart. Puglia's landscape is as varied as it is interesting, with a wide range of breathtaking scenery.

Consider yourself standing on the Adriatic Sea's coast, with its glittering blue waves and beautiful beaches stretching out in front of you. To the west, the Ionian Sea offers a distinct shoreline experience, complete with isolated coves and charming fishing villages.

The Salento Peninsula, hidden between these two oceans, begs to be explored with its golden beaches, olive farms, and wineries. As you go farther inland, you'll come across rolling hills lined with olive trees, which produce some of the best olive oil in Italy. This breathtaking environment is studded with charming towns and villages, each with its own personality and history.

Let us now look at Puglia's climate. Consider living in a Mediterranean paradise where the sun shines for the majority of the year. Puglia's Mediterranean climate provides mild, wet winters and hot, dry summers. From late April to early October, the region's outdoor activities are best enjoyed on sunny days.

Summers in Puglia are sunny and pleasant, making them excellent for sunning on beaches, touring historical sites, and indulging in regional cuisine. However, keep in mind that temperatures can suddenly rise, so staying hydrated and seeking shade during the hottest parts of the day is a good idea.

The weather is milder in autumn and spring, making them excellent for outdoor activities like hiking, cycling, and exploring Puglia's natural beauty. Even in winter, there is beauty; while certain attractions may have shortened hours, you can still enjoy the local culture, gourmet delights, and year-round events.

It's worth mentioning that, while the weather in Puglia is normally good, it can be unpredictable at times. It's a good idea to pack clothing and check the weather forecast before venturing out for the day.

Traveling across Puglia's unique landscape and enjoying its lovely weather, you'll learn that each corner of this region has something new and exciting to offer. Puglia's varied topography and pleasant climate will ensure that your voyage is full of surprises, whether you're relaxing on the beaches, hiking through nature trails, or exploring old villages.

1.3 Historical and Cultural Background

As you travel to Puglia, it is vital to comprehend the rich cultural and historical fabric that has shaped this region into the captivating destination that it is today. The history of Puglia is an exciting tale of civilizations, conquests, and cultural exchanges that have left an indelible impression on the region's identity.

Consider walking through the streets of Lecce, where exquisite Baroque architecture pays tribute to the artistic prowess of the past. This city, renowned as the "Florence of the South," has a unique blend of architectural styles influenced by several historical periods.

Puglia has a long history, with Greek and Roman influences reflected in the region's historic sites. As you visit the Archaeological Park of Egnazia, you'll travel back in time to the ancient city of Gnathia, where remnants of its history await your discovery.

During the Middle Ages, Puglia witnessed the construction of outstanding castles such as Castel del Monte, a UNESCO World Heritage Site. Emperor Frederick II built this octagonal fortress, which is a marvel of medieval architecture that continues to astonish visitors.

Despite being in the neighboring area of Basilicata, Matera is a must-see for its breathtaking "Sassi" - rock-hewn buildings that were originally dwellings carved into the rock. This unique UNESCO World Heritage Site offers a glimpse into a way of life that has evolved over millennia.

The culture of Puglia is as diverse and intriguing as its history. Every event, from the raucous folk song and dance of the Notte della Taranta festival to the reverence displayed during the Feast of Saint Oronzo in Lecce, provides a glimpse into the local character.

The cuisine of Puglia is also an essential part of its culture. The region's agricultural heritage, along with its seaside location, has resulted in a gourmet tapestry that is as rich as it is delightful. Consider indulging in world-famous burrata cheese, enjoying the simplicity of orecchiette pasta, and savoring the earthy delights of locally produced olive oil.

Every cobblestone street, historic structure, and dish you eat has layers of history and culture that have been cultivated over decades. Puglia's past is alive in the people, traditions, and real feeling of pride that you will encounter on your journey, not just in museums.

So, while you travel to Puglia's lovely villages, attend cultural events, and sample the region's superb cuisine, you'll have a greater knowledge of the region's rich heritage. Every step you take is an opportunity to become a part of this vibrant living history, transforming your trip to Puglia into a journey into the heart and soul of a captivating culture.

1.4 Local Food and Wine

Let us now tantalize your taste buds by delving into the wonderful world of Puglia's distinctive cuisine and wine. Puglia isn't just a scenic feast; it's also a foodie's paradise, offering a diverse and delightful gourmet experience.

Consider yourself seated at a rustic table in a charming trattoria, ready for a culinary adventure. Puglia's cuisine is deeply rooted in its agricultural heritage and coastal prosperity, resulting in dishes that embody both land and sea. Burrata cheese, a creamy delight that is sure to impress, is one of the region's culinary treasures.

Consider the love and care that went into crafting this simple yet exquisite dish as you enjoy each piece of orecchiette pasta. This pasta is fashioned like little ears and is typically served with a variety of delicious sauces.

When it comes to sauces, Puglia is famous for its robust tomato-based sauces. The tomatoes used in Puglian cuisine are nothing short of remarkable, whether you're creating a hearty ragù or a simple pomodoro sauce.

Not to mention the famed olive oil from the region. Puglia is the top olive oil producer in Italy, and its golden elixir is a household staple. Spread this liquid gold on warm toast or use it to enhance the flavors of your foods. The flavor is astounding, perfectly capturing the spirit of Puglian terroir.

Let us now discuss wine. For years, wine has been produced in Puglia's vineyards, and the region has a rich viticultural tradition. There are several indigenous grape varieties that have grown in the climate and soil of Puglia.

The powerful Primitivo red wine is a true Puglian star, with deep flavors and aromas of black fruit. The Negroamaro vine, on the other hand, produces wines that are as exceptional, with a spice that will pique your curiosity.

When you taste a glass of Puglian wine, you are immersed in the region's history and the craftsmanship of generations. Many wineries provide tours and tastings, which allow you to witness the winemaking process firsthand.

So, when you explore Puglia's towns, beaches, and historical sites, keep the region's specialties in mind. Each course and wine taste will transport you to the heart of Puglia, leaving you with a deep appreciation for the gastronomic riches that make this region so unique.

Travel Requirements

2.1 Travel Planning

This section is dedicated to providing you with the materials you need to plan a seamless and memorable vacation to Puglia. You'll find important information here to help you make informed decisions and make sure your vacation arrangements exactly match your preferences and interests. This section will guide you through the planning phase of your Puglia trip, from identifying the best time to visit to understanding entrance processes. Let's get started and learn about the most crucial aspects of planning a trip to this amazing location.

2.1.1 When Is the Best Time to Visit?

The optimal time to visit Puglia is essential for getting the most of your trip. Puglia's attractions and activities change with the seasons, so understanding the seasonal nuances might help you tailor your vacation to your interests.

Spring (March-May): Spring is a beautiful time to visit Puglia. The landscape comes alive with flowering flowers and magnificent vistas as the weather warms. It's ideal for outdoor activities like hiking and cycling, as well as viewing historical sites without the summer crowds.

Summer (June to August): The summer months in Puglia are marked by warm weather and a lively environment. This is peak tourist season, so many people flock to the beaches and towns. Swimming is appealing, and the region's festivals and festivities are in full swing. Warmer temperatures and a buzzing, energetic environment are to be expected.

Autumn (September to November): Autumn is a great time to visit Puglia because the weather is still nice and the summer crowds have thinned. The region is still lush, making now an excellent time to harvest wine and olive oil. Cultural events continue during this season, providing a more relaxed and authentic experience.

While Puglia enjoys warmer winters than many other destinations, this is the off-season for tourists. This can be beneficial for guests looking for a more intimate, calmer experience. Even if particular attractions and restaurants have limited hours, you can still enjoy the local culture and cuisine.

Finally, the best time to visit Puglia depends on your preferences. Each season has its own special attraction, whether you're seeking for colorful festivals, calm beaches, or lonely exploration. Remember that hotels and attractions may be more crowded during the summer months, so planning ahead of time and considering your interests will help you make the most of your Puglia trip.

2.1.2 Suggestions for Stay Duration

The length of your stay in Puglia is crucial for getting the most out of your vacation and discovering the region's many alternatives. Your interests, travel pace, and level of investigation will all influence the recommended time. Consider the following timing suggestions:

Short Getaway (3 to 5 Days): If you don't have much time, a short getaway will allow you to experience the sights of Puglia. Concentrate on one or two significant places, such as visiting Bari and Alberobello or immersing oneself in Lecce culture. Keep in mind that, due to the limited time available, you will need to focus on select attractions.

Weeklong Retreat (7 to 10 Days): A week offers a more in-depth experience, with the ability to visit different towns and places. You might go from Bari to the Salento Peninsula, stopping in places like Ostuni, Polignano a Mare, and Gallipoli. This time allows you to immerse yourself in the local culture, relax on the beach, and sample the cuisine.

Extended Journey (10+ Days): If you have more than a week, you can delve deeper into Puglia's alternatives. Off-the-beaten-path destinations like Gargano National Park or day trips to lesser-known communities could be included. This time frame also allows for flexibility and leisure, allowing you to fully immerse yourself in the region's ambiance.

Remember that Puglia's many attractions cater to a wide range of interests, whether history, beaches, culinary experiences, or a combination of the two. Whatever amount of time you pick, personalizing your itinerary to your preferences will ensure that your visit to Puglia is both enriching and pleasurable.

2.1.3 Itinerary for 7 Days

7-Day Puglia Discovery Itinerary - Discovering the Essence of the Region

Day 1: Arrival in Bari

Arrive at Karol Wojtya International Airport in Bari.

Check into your preferred Bari lodging.

Explore Bari's historic center, featuring the Basilica di San Nicola and Castello Svevo.

Enjoy a traditional Apulian meal at a local trattoria.

Day 2: Exploration of Bari and Polignano a Mare

A early excursion to Bari's busy Mercato Coperto.

Discover Polignano a Mare, a beach town known for its breathtaking cliffside setting.

Enjoy lunch by the sea while gazing out at the crystal-clear seas.

Return to Bari and lunch at a well-known restaurant.

Day 3: Alberobello and Locorotondo

Visit Alberobello, known for its Trulli houses. Look into the Trulli district.

Continue on to Locorotondo, a white-brick circular arrangement.

Have lunch at a local eatery in Locorotondo.

Return to Bari in the evening to relax.

Day 4: Otranto and Lecce

Travel to Lecce, known as "Southern Florence," to discover its Baroque buildings and medieval streets.

Lunch in a traditional Lecce restaurant.

Continue on to Otranto, known for its stunning mosaic church floor.

Enjoy a relaxed supper by the water in Otranto.

Day 5: Gallipoli and Salento beaches

Gallipoli, with its lovely old town and beautiful beaches, is visited in the morning.

Relax on the beaches of Torre Lapillo, which have crystal-clear waters.

Return to your hotel for a restful evening.

Day 6: Ostuni and Cisternino

Discover the "White City" of Ostuni, with its white-washed streets.

Cisternino is notable for its winding alleyways and historic houses.

Enjoy a traditional meal in Cisternino's gorgeous setting.

Day 7: Departure from Castel del Monte

Visit Castel del Monte, a UNESCO World Heritage site known for its octagonal shape.

Depending on your departure time, have one last Apulian dinner.

Return to the Karol Wojtya Airport in Bari with happy memories of Puglia.

Please keep in mind that while this itinerary provides a comprehensive overview of Puglia's attractions, you are free to modify it to your individual interests and preferences. Furthermore, especially during peak seasons, confirm the opening hours and availability of attractions ahead of time.

2.1.4 Visa and Entry Requirements

It is vital to understand the visa and entry processes before traveling to Puglia to ensure a smooth entry into Italy and the province. While residents of the European Union (EU) usually have easy entry, travelers from other countries should keep the following in mind:

EU Citizens: You can go to Puglia if you are an EU citizen with a valid passport or national ID card. There is no need for a visa, and you can stay for up to 90 days within a 180-day period. Check sure your documents are still valid for the duration of your visit.

Non-EU Citizens: Non-EU citizens may be needed to obtain a Schengen visa in order to enter Italy and Puglia. This visa allows you to travel inside the Schengen Area for up to 90 days in a 180-day period. To find out if you need a visa and how to apply, contact the Italian consulate or embassy in your country.

Passport Validity: Regardless of nationality, your passport should be valid for at least six months after your anticipated departure date from Italy.

Remember that entry requirements can change, so double-check with the relevant authorities or official websites before your departure date. Having the necessary papers and understanding the visa requirements will allow you to embark on your Puglia adventure with confidence.

2.1.5 Travel Protection

Travel insurance is an essential element of planning your trip to Puglia since it protects you in the event of an unexpected disaster. While visiting the beauty of Puglia, having the correct travel insurance can give you peace of mind and financial protection.

Here are some of the reasons why travel insurance is essential:

Medical Coverage: Travel insurance typically covers medical emergencies, doctor visits, hospital stays, and medicines. This is especially important while traveling abroad, where healthcare costs may be prohibitively expensive.

Cancellation and Interruption of Vacation: Life is unpredictable, and unexpected occurrences may force you to cancel or curtail your vacation. Travel insurance can reimburse you for non-refundable expenses such as flights, hotel, and tours in the event of a trip cancellation or interruption.

Luggage Lost or Delayed: Imagine arriving in Puglia only to learn that your luggage has not arrived. Travel insurance can protect you against lost, stolen, or delayed luggage, ensuring you don't go without essentials.

Travel Delays: If your flights are delayed due to weather, mechanical issues, or other circumstances, travel insurance can reimburse you for additional expenses such as hotel and meals.

Travel insurance typically includes 24-hour emergency assistance, which can be essential if you are in a challenging situation away from home.

When choosing travel insurance, make sure you:

Carefully read the policy specifics to understand what is and is not covered.

Consider the level of coverage you need based on your vacation's activities and duration.

Confirm sure the insurance covers Puglia and Italy explicitly.

Carry a copy of your insurance policy and emergency contact information with you at all times.

Travel insurance adds an added layer of security to your trip, allowing you to concentrate on having fun in Puglia rather than worrying about unforeseen setbacks. It's a small investment that can make a significant difference if anything unexpected occurs.

2.2 How to Get to Puglia

2.2.1 Air Travel

Flying to Puglia is a quick and convenient method to visit this lovely region. Puglia has numerous airports, making it accessible from both Italy and a range of international locations. Here is a comprehensive list of Puglia flight alternatives:

Bari Karol Wojtya Airport (BRI): Located in Bari, this airport serves as the primary gateway to Puglia. It is a popular destination for vacationers because it offers a wide range of domestic and international flights. The airport provides easy access to the main heart of Bari as well as other nearby cities.

Brindisi Papola Casale Airport (BDS): Another major entry point into Puglia is provided by this airport in Brindisi. It serves a number of domestic and international destinations. From Brindisi Airport, the Salento Peninsula and its magnificent cities are easily accessible.

Airport Transportation: When you arrive at the airport, you will find a number of transportation options to get you to your destination. Taxis, private transportation, and shuttle services are available from the airports to various parts of Puglia. Some big cities also have train stations that can be reached by shuttle or cab.

International Connections: If you are traveling from another country, direct flights from major European cities to Bari or Brindisi are available. Connecting flights via major European hubs are particularly popular, providing you with extra alternatives when organizing your trip.

Domestic Flights: If you're already in Italy, you can simply get to Puglia by taking a domestic flight from another major Italian city. Bari and Brindisi airports are well connected to major Italian airports.

Renting a Car: Renting a car is the best way to see Puglia's vast network of cities, beaches, and attractions. Many international and domestic car rental firms have offices at airports, allowing you to pick up your vehicle and start your Puglia adventure immediately upon arrival.

Local Transportation: Once in Puglia, you can explore the region further by taking advantage of local transportation options such as buses and trains. Buses provide a trustworthy way of transportation between towns, whilst trains provide a comfortable mode of transportation across longer distances.

Puglia's well-connected airports ensure that you can easily begin your tour of this fascinating region, whether you arrive from another Italian city or from abroad. Your journey across Puglia's rich history, culture, and landscapes starts here.

2.2.2 Travel via Train

Rail travel in Puglia is not only convenient, but also a scenic and comfortable way to explore the region. Puglia's train network is well-connected, giving easy options for both domestic and foreign passengers. Here's all you need to know about train travel in Puglia:

Significant Train Stations: Puglia is home to a number of major train stations that serve as regional transit centers. The train station in Bari Centrale and the train station in Lecce are two of the busiest, with connections to sites throughout Puglia and beyond.

Domestic Connections: Puglia's train network connects significant towns and cities inside the region, making it simple to travel between cities such as Bari, Lecce, Brindisi, and Taranto. Trains are a popular means of transportation for both locals and visitors due to their convenience and accessibility.

Intercity and Regional Trains: The Italian train system includes intercity and regional trains. Intercity trains are faster and frequently provide direct connections between major cities, but regional trains stop frequently and are ideal for visiting smaller towns and scenic areas.

International Connections: If you are going from outside of Europe, you can reach Puglia via major Italian towns via the extensive train network. The smooth travel provided by connected trains allows you to enjoy the beautiful Italian scenery along the way.

Tickets for trains can be purchased online, at the station, or through travel agencies. It is essential to purchase your tickets in advance for popular routes, especially during peak travel seasons.

Comfort and amenities: In Italy, trains range in comfort from basic to luxurious. On some trains, dining carriages, power outlets, and Wi-Fi are offered. First-class tickets are more spacious and comfortable.

Local Attractions: Traveling by train allows you to explore all of Puglia's scenery, from coastline views to rolling countryside. You can also strike up conversations with locals and other travelers to add a cultural component to your experience.

Transfers and Local Transportation: Once you arrive, you can use local transportation such as buses, trams, and taxis to travel to your accommodation or to explore more.

Traveling by train in Puglia allows you to not only relax and enjoy the scenery, but it also provides a real look into the region's daily life. Train travel, with its quick connections and pleasant accommodations, is a fantastic way to discover Puglia's treasures.

2.2.3 Travel to Puglia by Bus and Car

Traveling by bus or automobile in Puglia allows you to visit charming cities, rest on beaches, or explore the countryside at your leisure. The following is a comprehensive list of bus and automobile transportation options to Puglia:

Taking the bus:
Puglia has an extensive regional bus network that connects towns, cities, and even remote villages. These buses are a cheap way to travel between locations and explore places that may not be easily accessible by train.

Intercity buses connect major cities and towns in Puglia as well as the surrounding areas. They are an excellent choice for longer treks and less frequented locations.

Bus Stations: In large cities such as Bari, Lecce, and Brindisi, central bus stations give information on routes, schedules, and ticket transactions.

Tickets and schedules for buses are frequently available at the station or from the driver. It is advisable to double-check timetables ahead of time, particularly for less frequent routes.

When traveling by car:
Renting a Car: Renting a car in Puglia allows you to explore the region's grandeur off the usual path. At major airports and places, there are various car rental companies to select from.

Driving Conditions: Roads in Puglia are generally in good condition, and highways connect major towns and cities. Expect narrower streets in historic neighborhoods and rural areas, however.

When it comes to navigating the roads of Puglia, GPS devices and navigation software will be your best friends. Because the signage is in Italian, a reliable navigation device is required.

Parking: Most municipalities have designated parking lots, which are frequently fee-based during certain hours. Parking is available at certain accommodations.

Local Roads & stunning Routes: Puglia's local roads offer stunning views of the landscape and shore.

Consider driving scenic roads to properly appreciate the region's splendor.

Driving Instructions: Driving on the right side of the road is the norm in Italy. Remember to obey road laws, especially speed limits and parking regulations.

Whether you prefer the convenience of public transportation or the independence of driving, both provide unique experiences for visitors to Puglia. Traveling by bus allows you to relax and enjoy the scenery while someone else drives, whereas renting a car allows you to find hidden gems and create your own itinerary. Choose the mode of transportation that best suits your interests and travel style for a memorable Puglia experience.

Accommodation

3.1 Different Types of Accommodation

Puglia has a wide range of lodging options to suit a variety of budgets, preferences, and travel patterns. Puglia has something for everyone, whether you want luxury, authenticity, or a low-cost stay. Here's a rundown of the several types of lodging available:

Hotels: Puglia has a diverse range of hotels, from little gems to opulent resorts. Choose between modern accommodations with all the facilities you'd expect and historical palaces that immerse you in the region's history. Beachfront hotels with beautiful views are available in coastal areas, while city centers provide easy access to cultural landmarks.

Bed and Breakfast (B&B): B&Bs in Puglia provide a more personalized experience, as they are frequently hosted by locals who can provide insider insights and recommendations. Enjoy lovely lodgings, fresh meals, and the opportunity to meet other tourists.

Agriturismo: Agriturismos are rural lodgings that offer a genuine experience of Puglian life. These functioning farms frequently offer rooms or apartments to tourists, allowing you to get a firsthand look at local agriculture and gastronomy.

Trulli Accommodation: Stay in a traditional trullo to immerse yourself in the unique beauty of Puglia. These iconic cone-shaped structures provide snug and authentic lodging, ideal for a one-of-a-kind experience.

Masserias are antique fortified farmhouses that have been converted into magnificent lodgings. Enjoy rustic comfort, tranquil scenery, and a look into the region's rural past.

Holiday Apartments & Rentals: Renting an apartment or a house is a great option for families or larger parties. You'll be able to make your own meals and have a home-away-from-home experience.

Resorts and Villas: Puglia has a number of upmarket resorts and private villas for people seeking luxury. In gorgeous settings, enjoy first-rate amenities, spa facilities, and customized services.

Budget and Hostel Accommodations: On a tight budget? Look for low-cost hotels and hostels that offer clean and uncomplicated options for quiet nights.

Booking Platforms: There are numerous internet platforms that allow you to search for and book hotels in Puglia. Examine reviews, photos, and descriptions to confirm that your chosen accomodation meets your expectations.

Considerations for Location: The type of accommodation you choose may vary depending on your preferred destinations and activities. Coastal accommodations are perfect for beach leisure, while downtown hotels are ideal for city exploration.

Whatever sort of accommodation you choose, Puglia's numerous offers ensure that your stay is comfortable and suited to your preferences. Puglia's accommodations are ready to welcome you with open arms, whether you seek rustic realism, opulent indulgence, or everything in between.

3.1.1 Resorts and Hotels

Puglia has a profusion of superb hotels and resorts that cater to a wide range of interests and inclinations. Here are some top-notch options to consider for your stay in Puglia, whether you're searching for lavish accommodation, historical charm, or beachfront relaxation:

Borgo Egnazia, Fasano: A luxury resort that embodies Puglian architecture's charm. It's ideal for people looking for upmarket comfort, with a private beach, golf courses, and a spa.

Masseria Torre Coccaro, Savelletri di Fasano: This quaint masseria turned luxury hotel combines rustic authenticity with modern comfort, including a private beach club.

Palazzo Bozzi Corso, Lecce: An tastefully constructed boutique hotel in the center of Lecce with convenient access to the city's historic sights.

Relais La Sommità, Ostuni: Perched on a hill overlooking the city of Ostuni, this contemporary hotel offers panoramic views, sumptuous amenities, and a well-regarded restaurant.

Don Ferrante, Monopoli: A boutique hotel within the old walls of Monopoli, giving stunning views of the Adriatic Sea and an intimate setting.

VOI Tanka Village, Villasimius: Located in Sardinia, this family-friendly resort has a sibling site in Puglia, VOI Alimini Resort. Enjoy a variety of pools, entertainment, and beach access.

Canne Bianche Lifestyle Hotel, Torre Canne: This hotel provides a modern and elegant beachside experience, as well as a spa and wellness center.

Grand Hotel La Chiusa di Chietri, Alberobello: This hotel in the countryside in Alberobello offers a tranquil location with a spa, pool, and wellness center.

Le Alcove Luxury Hotel Nei Trulli, Alberobello: Immerse yourself in trullo living by staying at this one-of-a-kind luxury hotel with specially built rooms located in historic trulli.

Masseria Cervarolo, Ostuni: This masseria, nestled in the countryside, offers a calm refuge with magnificent grounds, a pool, and great dining.

Consider variables such as location, amenities, and the overall experience you seek when selecting a hotel or resort. The numerous offerings of Puglia ensure that you'll discover the proper lodging to make your stay memorable and comfortable.

3.1.2 Hotels with Bed and Breakfast

Puglia's Bed and Breakfasts (B&Bs) provide a personalized and delightful experience, frequently hosted by locals who share insights into the region's culture and hidden jewels. Here are some excellent B&B options in Puglia that provide a pleasant and authentic stay:

Bed & Breakfast Palazzo de Giorgi, Lecce: Housed in

a medieval castle in Lecce's city center, this magnificent B&B offers beautifully appointed rooms and a warm, welcoming ambiance.

Dimora Rossi B&B, Polignano a Mare: Located in a classic stone structure, this B&B offers comfortable rooms and a convenient location just steps from Polignano a Mare's magnificent shore.

La Fiermontina Urban Resort, Lecce: This urban resort combines the charm of a B&B with the luxury of a boutique hotel, featuring a pool, a garden, and an art-filled decor.

Bed & Breakfast Vittorio Emanuele, Ostuni: Located in the ancient core of Ostuni, this B&B offers pleasant rooms with traditional décor and convenient access to the town's attractions.

B&B La Stazione, Conversano: Located in a former railway station, this B&B offers unusual accommodations as well as a nice garden in which to unwind.

Borgo Antico Santa Lucia, Monopoli: Located in a restored property in Monopoli, this B&B offers nice accommodations as well as a convenient location near the coast.

Il Viottolo B&B, Alberobello: Immerse yourself in the

trulli lifestyle at this B&B, which offers authentic trulli rooms as well as a calm garden.

Il Giardino dei Pini B&B, Torre Canne: Surrounded by pine trees, this B&B offers a calm retreat near the beach as well as a friendly and helpful ambiance.

Masseria Baroni Nuovi B&B, Fasano: Stay in a delightful masseria with rustic yet magnificent apartments, a pool, and the opportunity to immerse yourself in the authentic Puglian countryside.

Tenuta Centoporte B&B, Otranto: This B&B offers a relaxing ambiance, a pool, and convenient access to Otranto's historical monuments.

Consider features such as location, the host's hospitality, and the property's distinctive appeal when choosing a B&B. B&Bs offer a more personal experience, allowing you to interact with people and create memorable experiences during your stay in Puglia.

3.1.3 Agriturismo (Farm Stays)

Staying at an agriturismo (farm stay) in Puglia provides a once-in-a-lifetime opportunity to immerse oneself in rural life, eat fresh local produce, and experience genuine hospitality. Here are some remarkable Puglia agriturismos that offer a true experience of the region's agricultural heritage:

Masseria Montenapoleone, Pezze di Greco: This magnificent agriturismo provides beautifully refurbished accommodations, a pool, and delicious farm-to-table cuisine.

Masseria Spina Resort, Monopoli: With comfortable rooms, a pool, and a focus on local cuisine, this quaint masseria offers a blend of tradition and modernity.

Masseria Potenti, Manduria: This masseria offers wine tastings, a pool, and nice lodgings in a beautiful setting surrounded by wineries.

Masseria Il Frantoio, Ostuni: This old masseria offers cooking instruction, a wellness center, and nice rooms, as well as direct access to olive oil manufacturing.

Masseria Le Fabriche, Fasano: This agriturismo offers a peaceful setting, an outdoor pool, and meals made from locally produced ingredients.

Masseria Cappotto in Carovigno produces olive oil, wine, and other items. Stay in beautiful rooms, unwind by the pool, and eat traditional dishes.

Azienda Agrituristica Masseria La Brunetta, Tricase:

Located in the heart of Salento, this agriturismo provides a variety of activities, including olive oil tastings and farm excursions.

Azienda Agrituristica Masseria Torre Sant'Andrea, Melendugno: This agriturismo gives convenient access to the sea as well as comfortable rooms.

Masseria Santa Teresa, Sava: This rustic masseria offers charming rooms, a pool, and a true Puglian farm experience complete with olive groves and vineyards.

Masseria Lamacavallo, Monopoli: Surrounded by nature, this agriturismo offers peace and quiet, a pool, and the opportunity to tour the farm and eat home-cooked meals.

Agriturismos are an excellent way to connect with the land, culture, and people of Puglia. Each hotel provides a distinctive experience, ranging from wine tastings to cooking workshops, ensuring that your stay is both enlightening and unforgettable.

3.1.4 Vacation Rentals

Choosing a holiday rental or apartment in Puglia allows you to set your own schedule and enjoy a home-away-from-home experience. Here are some good holiday rentals in Puglia that provide convenience, comfort, and the opportunity to immerse oneself in local life:

Alberobello's Trullo Azzurro: Stay in a historic trullo with modern conveniences, a private pool, and a tranquil countryside setting.

Apartment Corte Regina, Lecce: This delightful apartment is located in the ancient core of Lecce and provides convenient access to the city's sights, restaurants, and shops.

property Pizzorusso, Ostuni: A spacious property with a pool and grounds that is ideal for families or parties looking for a peaceful escape near Ostuni.

Casa De Donno, Polignano a Mare: This small apartment is just feet from the water, allowing you to fully appreciate Polignano a Mare's coastline beauty.

Borgo San Rocco Apartment, Gallipoli: Located in the heart of Gallipoli's historic district, this apartment provides a comfortable base for exploring the town's attractions.

Trullo Ventura, Cisternino: Combine the rustic beauty of a trullo with modern conveniences such as a pool and spectacular views of the surrounding countryside.

property Belvedere, Monopoli: A lovely property with magnificent sea views, a pool, and a private terrace.

property Blu Mare, Santa Maria al Bagno: This coastal property offers beautiful sea views as well as convenient access to the beach and local services.

Trullo del Bosco, Martina Franca: This trullo set in a woodland provides solitude and a one-of-a-kind retreat.

House Sofia in Torre Canne: A beachfront house with a private pool, gardens, and direct access to the Adriatic Sea.

Holiday rentals allow you to explore Puglia at your own leisure, prepare your own meals, and relax in the seclusion of your own home. Whether you're searching for a romantic getaway, a family-friendly retreat, or a get-together with friends, Puglia's holiday rentals offer the ideal location for a memorable stay.

3.2 Selecting the Best Accommodation

3.2.1 Considerations for Location

Choosing the proper location for your Puglia accommodation is critical to determining your overall experience. Puglia has a broad spectrum of scenery, from coastal towns to rural getaways, each with their own distinct appeal. Here are some significant location factors to consider before making a decision:

Coastal Delights: If the charm of the sea draws you in, consider staying in coastal cities like Polignano a Mare, Ostuni, Monopoli, or Gallipoli. These locations provide beach access, aquatic sports, and stunning vistas.

Historic City Centers: Stay in the heart of historic city centers such as Lecce, Bari, and Alberobello. This option provides convenient access to cultural sites, shopping, restaurants, and a thriving local life.

Farms Retreats: Stay in a masseria, agriturismo, or trullo to immerse yourself in the tranquility of Puglia's farms. These locations provide tranquil scenery, real experiences, and opportunities to interact with nature.

Puglia is filled with lovely communities that provide an intimate peek into local life. For an off-the-beaten-path adventure, consider vacationing in Locorotondo, Cisternino, or Martina Franca.

Proximity to sites: Select lodgings that are conveniently positioned near the sites you want to visit. This might save you time on the road and allow you to make the most of your itinerary.

Consider the accessibility of transportation options such as railway stations, bus stops, and main roadways. This is especially vital if you intend to visit several locations throughout your stay.

Beach vs. countryside: Consider if you prefer the vibrant vibe of coastal communities or the tranquil ambience of farming. Both provide distinct experiences, so choose based on your preferred pace.

Personal Interests: Match your area to your interests. Staying in a historic city may be ideal if you enjoy history. A countryside holiday could be excellent if you enjoy nature.

Local Culture: Staying in lodgings that represent the region's heritage, such as trulli, masserias, or agriturismos, is a great way to immerse oneself in

Puglian culture.

Accessibility: If you're arriving by plane or train, look for hotels that are conveniently located to save down on journey time.

You can choose the finest location for your Puglia hotel by carefully evaluating your tastes, interests, and desired experiences. Keep in mind that Puglia's numerous choices ensure that you can choose a suitable location that matches your travel goals.

3.2.2 Budget-Friendly Alternatives

Exploring Puglia on a budget doesn't have to mean foregoing comfort or unique experiences. There are numerous budget-friendly lodging options that offer value without sacrificing quality. Here are some fantastic options for budget-conscious visitors to Puglia:

Ostuni Rosa Marina Resort, Ostuni: This low-cost resort has pleasant rooms, a pool, and beach access, making it an excellent alternative for families and beachgoers.

Hotel Residence Laurito, Polignano a Mare: This residence offers affordable rooms in a comfortable location, just a short distance from the shore.

Hotel Europa, Bari: Located near the ancient heart of

Bari, this hotel offers affordable rooms within walking distance of the city's main attractions.

B&B La Muraglia, Lecce: This charming B&B offers reasonably priced rooms in a handy location, allowing you to immerse yourself in the rich culture of Lecce.

Hotel Piccolo Mondo, Alberobello: Relax at this reasonably priced hotel located near Alberobello's iconic trulli.

B&B Villa Ernestina, Gallipoli: This B&B provides cheap lodgings with a calm garden, allowing you to relax after a day of exploring Gallipoli.

Hotel Villaggio Cala Corvino, Polignano a Mare: This beachfront hotel offers affordable rooms, direct access to the sea, and close proximity to the attractions of Polignano a Mare.

B&B Santa Maria al Bagno, Nard: Enjoy a low-cost stay at this B&B, which is located near the beach and has a pleasant ambiance.

B&B Le Vedute, Martina Franca: This B&B offers budget-friendly accommodations with panoramic views of the Valle d'Itria, allowing you to explore the countryside on the cheap.

B&B Santa Chiara, Conversano: Stay in a beautiful B&B in the ancient center of Conversano without breaking the budget.

These low-cost options allow you to discover Puglia without breaking the bank, ensuring that your vacation is pleasurable and memorable. While on a budget, these lodgings still give comfortable stays and easy access to Puglia's attractions.

3.2.3 Luxurious Accommodations

Puglia provides a variety of opulent hotel options that promise opulence, top-notch services, and unforgettable experiences for those looking for the utmost indulgence and pampering. Here are some fantastic luxury accommodations in Puglia that will satisfy your craving for opulence and sophistication:

Borgo Egnazia, Fasano: This large resort offers beautiful suites, a championship golf course, a private beach, and a well-known spa.

Masseria Torre Coccaro, Savelletri di Fasano: This beautiful masseria features a spa, golf course, private beach club, and great dining.

Don Ferrante, Monopoli: Enjoy the beauty of a boutique luxury hotel with spectacular sea views, a rooftop patio, and exceptional service at Don Ferrante.

Masseria Cimino, Ostuni: For an exceptional visit, this beautifully restored masseria provides exclusive rooms, a calm pool, and an intimate ambiance.

La Fiermontina Urban Resort, Lecce: This urban resort combines modern elegance with historical charm, featuring a private pool, art-filled interiors, and exquisite service.

Masseria Pettolecchia, Monopoli: This lovely masseria offers luxury in the midst of olive orchards, replete with a pool, wellness center, and gourmet cuisine.

Masseria Le Carrube, Gallipoli: This lovely masseria features elegant rooms, a pool, and breathtaking views of the Ionian Sea.

Tenuta Centoporte, Otranto: Refresh your senses at this luxury resort, which features a spa, pool, and attractively designed rooms near the picturesque town of Otranto.

Masseria San Domenico, Savelletri di Fasano: With a golf course, spa, and direct access to the sea, this beautiful masseria combines traditional elegance with modern luxury.

Masseria Prosperi, Fasano: Immerse yourself in the

elegance of this magnificently renovated masseria surrounded by olive trees, complete with a spa, pool, and gourmet dining.

These luxury accommodations provide a blend of opulence, comfort, and remarkable experiences that will make your visit to Puglia absolutely unforgettable. Puglia's luxury hotels cater to your every need, whether it's a luxurious spa treatment, delicious cuisine, or simply the joy of being surrounded by refined beauty.

3.3 Reservation Resources and Platforms

Choosing the best Puglia hotel requires careful planning and booking through reputable websites. Here are some reservation suggestions and resources to help you make a successful booking:

Pre-book: Puglia is a popular destination, especially during high seasons. Make reservations well in advance to ensure your preferred lodging, especially for distinctive buildings such as trulli or masserias.

Consider having flexible travel times if at all possible. This can provide you with additional options and possibly reduced rates, as costs change according to the season.

Research and Reviews: Read reviews and gather information about the accommodations you've chosen. Websites such as TripAdvisor, Google Reviews, and travel forums can provide useful feedback from previous visitors.

Many hotels, bed and breakfasts, and agriturismos have official websites where you can book directly. Booking directly with the resort may occasionally provide additional benefits or special promotions.

Online Booking Platforms: Popular platforms such as Booking.com, Expedia, and Hotels.com provide a diverse selection of lodgings, user reviews, and simple booking methods. You can narrow down the results based on your interests.

Websites that aggregate pricing from numerous booking platforms, such as Trivago and Kayak, might help you locate the best value for your preferred hotel.

Agriturismo Platforms: For agriturismos, try using Agriturismo.it, which focuses on farm stays and rural accommodations.

Websites for Villa Rentals: If you're looking for villa rentals, websites like HomeAway and Airbnb let you explore and book villas that match your preferences.

Contact the Property: If you have any specific requests or questions, please contact the property directly by email or phone. They can give you reliable information and personalized advice.

Before making a reservation, check the cancellation policy, payment conditions, and any additional fees. This ensures that you are aware of the regulations in the event that they need to be changed.

Rate Comparison: Compare rates from several websites to verify you're getting the greatest bargain. Prices can vary between booking websites at times.

Travel companies: If you want, you may also employ Puglia-specific travel companies or tour operators to assist you in finding and reserving hotels.
You may reserve the appropriate lodging for your Puglia trip with confidence and convenience if you follow these reservation recommendations and use reputable booking platforms.

Cultural Experiences

Immerse yourself in Puglia's unique cultural tapestry, where centuries-old customs, enthralling history, and vibrant local life collide to offer a truly authentic and unforgettable experience. We encourage you to explore the varied spectrum of cultural encounters that await you in Puglia in this chapter. Puglia offers a plethora of options to interact with its past and create memorable memories, from historic buildings and local festivals to traditional crafts and culinary pleasures. Puglia's cultural experiences will reveal insights into the heart and spirit of this interesting area, whether you're roaming through ancient cities, eating local cuisine, or partaking in age-old customs. Join us on a journey that honors the past while embracing the present, all set against the enthralling backdrop of Puglia's own cultural character.

4.1 Community Festivals and Events

4.1.1 San Nicola's Feast

La Festa di San Nicola is an attractive celebration honoring Saint Nicholas, the adored patron saint of

Bari and guardian of mariners. This festival is both a religious celebration and a colorful cultural extravaganza that draws both residents and tourists. The event honors the saint with religious processions, ancient ceremonies, and exuberant festivities in Bari, the capital of Puglia.

Saint Nicholas, also known as San Nicola in Italian, is a beloved figure in Bari due to his historic ties to the city. He is supposed to have saved seafarers and performed miracles, making him a symbol of safety and good will. The celebration, held on May 7th and 8th, remembers his life and actions, and invites others to attend.

Highlights and Memories: Religious Processions: The celebration centres around grandiose processions that transport Saint Nicholas' statue through the streets of Bari. The monument is paraded through the city on a beautiful carriage, accompanied by religious hymns, prayers, and a sense of reverence.

Basilica di San Nicola: The event is centered on the Basilica di San Nicola, a gorgeous basilica that contains Saint Nicholas' remains. Pilgrims and visitors alike come to pay their respects and seek blessings at the basilica. The crypt containing the saint's relics is a popular place of worship.

Cultural Performances: In addition to religious festivities, the festival includes cultural performances, concerts, and traditional music, which add to the joyous atmosphere. Music, dancing, and local artists displaying their wares fill the city's squares and streets.

Fireworks: The festival concludes with a spectacular fireworks display that lights up the night sky over Bari's seafront. The spectacular show is a symbol of joy and solidarity, representing the event's common spirit.

Best Ways to Explore and Discover
Processions: Join the locals in religious processions to feel the passionate devotion and connect with the city's deeply ingrained rituals.

Explore the Basilica di San Nicola, both during the fair and throughout your stay in Bari. Admire the architecture, learn about the saint's life, and witness the city's close tie with its patron.

Engage with Locals: Engage in conversations with locals to understand about the festival's significance in their lives. They may share personal experiences and views regarding the festival's cultural significance.

Taste Traditional Food: Indulge in the regional

delicacies that are frequently cooked during the event. Taste Puglian cuisine and desserts to enhance your culinary experience.

Enjoy the Fireworks: Don't miss the spectacular fireworks display on May 8th. Find a vantage point along the waterfront to enjoy the spectacular show.

Nightlife: The event continues late into the evening with concerts and exciting nightlife. Immerse yourself in Bari's nightlife and revel in the celebratory atmosphere.

La Festa di San Nicola invites you to witness the heart and soul of Bari's identity through a compelling blend of religious reverence and cultural mirth. You will obtain a greater knowledge of the historical, spiritual, and celebratory components of this magnificent celebration by participating in the various activities and engaging with the local community.

4.1.2 Tarantella Night

Notte della Taranta is an exuberant celebration of the Pizzica dance and traditional music from Puglia's Salento region. This festival has evolved into a major cultural event, attracting music lovers and dancers from all over the world. Notte della Taranta, held every summer, is a colorful blend of music, dancing, and cultural heritage.

The festival is a resurrection of the ancient Pizzica Tarantata, a traditional dance believed to cure the mystical "taranta" spider bite by furious dancing. The goal of Notte della Taranta is to preserve and promote this cultural heritage while also accepting contemporary versions of Pizzica dance and music.

Highlights and Memories
Concerts & Performances: The festival includes a number of concerts and performances by well-known musicians and artists who come together to deliver enthralling versions of Pizzica music. The performances' intensity and enthusiasm are contagious.

Pizzica Dance courses: Attend dance courses to learn Pizzica dance routines and steps. Accept the happy atmosphere of the dance and immerse yourself in the rhythm.

The festival concludes with a spectacular finale concert, "La Notte della Taranta," hosted in Melpignano. This open-air concert draws large people and showcases stunning acts that celebrate the Pizzica dance's core.

Street Processions: Colorful processions fill the streets, with people dressed in traditional garb dancing and playing Pizzica music. Join the march to enjoy the event's communal atmosphere.

Local Crafts & food: During the event, visit the local craft markets and dine on authentic Salento food. Taste Puglia's specialties and revel in its flavors.

Best Ways to Explore and Discover
Attend the festival's concerts to experience the beauty of Pizzica music and dance. Allow the music to move you and observe the mix of classic and modern components.

Pizzica dance workshops allow you to master the rhythmic moves and experience the essence of the dance. It's a fantastic opportunity to engage with the music and culture.

Participate in Street Processions: To truly immerse yourself in the happy mood, take part in the colorful street processions. Celebrate the excitement of the Pizzica dance with residents and tourists alike.

Experience Melpignano: If possible, attend the festival's grand finale concert in Melpignano, when the energy and enthusiasm are at their pinnacle. Join the massive throng and be a part of this amazing occasion.

Explore Local Markets: Visit local craft markets to find unique artisanal products that exhibit the area's talent. Buy souvenirs and support local artisans.

Taste Local Cuisine: Indulge in traditional Salento cuisine and enjoy dishes from the region's culinary heritage. The event is a fantastic opportunity to sample the cuisine of Puglia.

The Notte della Taranta is a joyful and engaging event that invites you to dance, sing, and engage with the vibrant essence of Puglia's cultural identity. Participating in the performances, seminars, and vivid processions will allow you to become a part of this pulsing cultural phenomenon and create memories that echo with the heartbeats of the Salento region.

4.1.3 Saint Oronzo's Day

The Feast of Saint Oronzo, also known as the "Festa di Sant'Oronzo," is a joyous and historic feast honoring Saint Oronzo, the patron saint of Lecce. This event embodies the city's great religious devotion as well as its cultural history. The feast, which takes place every year on August 24th, transforms the picturesque streets of Lecce into a vivid display of traditions, processions, and festivities.

Origins and Importance: Saint Oronzo is revered as the guardian of Lecce, having saved the city from a locust epidemic during medieval times. The festival's origins can be traced back to the Middle Ages, when Lecce was in the grip of a severe drought, and the saint's intervention was thought to have preserved the city's harvests.

Highlights and Memories
Religious Procession: The festival's centerpiece is a solemn religious procession through the city streets, carrying the statue of Saint Oronzo. This procession is a religious display, with participants dressed in traditional garb and escorting the saint's statue.

Il Sedile: Witness the symbolic occasion of "Il Sedile," in which the mayor of Lecce presents the saint with a key as a token of gratitude. This tradition symbolizes the city's gratitude for Saint Oronzo's protection.

Luminarie: Luminarie, ornate and lit arches and decorations, enliven the streets of Lecce. These enthralling presentations create a wonderful atmosphere, especially when the sun sets.

Fireworks: The event finishes with a spectacular fireworks display that illuminates the night sky over Lecce. The fireworks serve as a joyful end to the feast, bringing together locals and tourists in wonder.

Traditional Music, Dance, and Performances: Traditional music, dance, and performances are featured throughout the event, adding to the celebratory ambiance. Folk music and dances from Puglia are performed, reflecting the region's traditional heritage.

Best Ways to Explore and Discover
Witness the march: Participate in the religious parade alongside the residents to experience the devotion and connect with the city's history. As you walk through the streets of Lecce, take in the artistically decorated monument of Saint Oronzo.

Explore the luminarie displays that adorn the city and admire the decorations. Take a stroll in the evening to see the streets come alive with entrancing lights and decorations.

Attend the "Il Sedile" event to witness the mayor's gesture of handing over the key to the city. Recognize the significance of this act of thankfulness.

Participate in Local Traditions: To fully immerse oneself in the joyful environment, embrace cultural events such as traditional music and dancing.

Enjoy the Fireworks: Don't miss the spectacular fireworks display that concludes the feast. Find a vantage point to see the beautiful hues that illuminate the night sky.

Discover Lecce: Take advantage of the festive atmosphere to explore the ancient sites, architecture, and local shops of Lecce. Immerse yourself in the distinctive charm of the city.

The Feast of Saint Oronzo provides an exceptional opportunity to experience Lecce's devotion to its patron saint while taking part in a raucous celebration of faith, culture, and community. Participating in the many activities and ceremonies will provide you with a better understanding of the city's history and cultural legacy, all set against the stunning backdrop of Lecce's charming streets.

4.2 Gastronomic Delights

4.2.1 Highlights of Puglian Cuisine

Introduction: The culinary environment of Puglia is a journey of flavors that captures the region's rich regions and coastal bounty. Puglian cuisine encourages you to indulge in a gastronomic experience that represents the region's cultural history and natural wealth, with a focus on simplicity, fresh ingredients, and time-honored techniques.

Highlights of Puglian Cuisine

1. Orecchiette avec Cime di Rapa: Orecchiette pasta is served with cime di rapa, which is a sort of broccoli rabe. This well-balanced combination of pasta and greens is frequently seasoned with olive oil, garlic, chili flakes, and a sprinkling of pecorino cheese.

2. Burrata: Burrata is a creamy cheese from Puglia. It has a creamy inside that pours out when sliced, providing a tasty contrast to the outside mozzarella shell. Serve with ripe tomatoes and fresh basil and drizzled with olive oil.

3. Focaccia Barese: Focaccia Barese is Puglia's version of focaccia, a soft and airy dough topped with cherry tomatoes, olives, oregano, and olive oil. It's a popular snack or antipasto.

4. Frisella: Frisella is a traditional Puglian bread that is twice baked for a delightful crunch. It's frequently soaked in water, drizzled with olive oil, and topped with tomatoes, herbs, and, on rare occasions, capers.

5. Puccia: Puccia is a circular, rustic bread that is cut open and stuffed with cured meats, cheese, vegetables, and olive oil. It's a tasty and portable supper option.

6. Polpo alla Pignata: Polpo alla Pignata is a rustic cuisine that consists of soft octopus slow-cooked in a clay pot with potatoes, tomatoes, peppers, and an aromatic herb combination. The end result is a thick and comforting seafood stew.

7. Taralli: Taralli are small, crunchy, and savory treats that come in a variety of tastes, including fennel, black pepper, and red pepper. They're ideal for snacking with a glass of local wine.

8. Pasticiotto Leccese: This delectable Lecce dish contains a flaky pastry filled with a creamy custard. It's a lovely way to end a Puglian meal.

9. Puglia is known for its superb olive oil, which is often referred to as "green gold." The region's olive orchards produce some of Italy's greatest extra virgin olive oils, which are liberally utilized in local recipes.

10. Local Wines: Pair your meals with the rich and strong Primitivo red wine or the crisp and refreshing Verdeca white wine from Puglia.

The Best Ways to Enjoy Puglian Cuisine
Visit authentic trattorias and local cafes to sample traditional Puglian meals prepared with passion and competence.

Visit local markets to find fresh produce, cheeses, olives, and other elements that define Puglian cuisine.

Cooking workshops: Take cooking workshops from local chefs who are concerned about maintaining culinary traditions to learn how to make Puglian delicacies.

Wine Tasting: Take wine tasting trips through Puglia's vineyards and cellar doors to experience the region's diverse wines.

Farm-to-Table Experiences: Participate in farm-to-table experiences to learn about Puglia's agricultural heritage, gather ingredients, and enjoy rustic-style meals.

By sampling Puglia's culinary highlights, you'll not only get to eat excellent food but also learn about the region's history, traditions, and the deep connection between its people and the land.

4.2.2 Olive Oil Taste Test

Introduction: Olive oil is the heart and soul of Puglian food, and it is a cornerstone of the region's culinary legacy. A trip to Puglia is incomplete unless you learn the art of olive oil tasting. This chapter welcomes you on a sensory voyage through the intricacies of Puglia's excellent olive oils, also known as "liquid gold."

Experience with Olive Oil Tasting

1. Understanding Varieties: Puglia is home to a variety of olive varieties, each of which contributes unique flavors and fragrances to the oils. Coratina, Ogliarola, and Leccino have distinct flavors ranging from peppery and robust to fruity and subtle.

2. Exploration of Terroir: Olive oil, like wine, is influenced by terroir—the soil, climate, and location in which the olives are grown. Puglia's several areas produce oils with distinct properties. To enjoy the effect of terroir, look for oils from the plains, hills, and coast.

3. scents and Flavors: During a tasting, you will be exposed to a variety of scents and flavors. Notes of fresh-cut grass, artichoke, green apple, almond, and a peppery finish can be found. The degree of these characteristics varies depending on the olive variety and ripeness.

4. To warm the oil slightly, use a tasting cup, a small spoon, or your palm. Deeply inhale to pick up on the smells, then take a little sip and let it coat your taste. In order to aerate the oil and boost its flavors, inhale some air.

5. Pairing Insights: Discover how to pair olive oils with various dishes. Robust oils are ideal for drizzling on salads, shellfish, and delicate pastas, while gentler oils are ideal for drizzling on salads, seafood, and delicate pastas.

6. Dipping Delight: Enjoy freshly baked bread dipped in a variety of olive oils. Take note of how different oils enhance the flavors of the bread and how your palate reacts to the interplay of textures.

7. Expert Advice: Take part in guided olive oil tastings led by local experts. They can give you information about the production process, olive types, and how to detect the minor nuances in each oil.

Best Ways to Enjoy Olive Oil Tasting
Visit olive oil mills (frantoi) in Puglia to see the production process and participate in guided tastings given by trained specialists.

Culinary Tours: Many culinary tours include olive oil tastings in their itineraries, providing a comprehensive experience that blends local food, wine, and olive oil.

Farm tours: Attend farm tours and agriturismo events, which frequently include olive oil tastings, to connect with the land and its produce.

specialist stores: Visit specialist stores and marketplaces dedicated to olive oil to obtain a curated collection of Puglian oils and customized guidance.

Cooking Classes: Enroll in cooking classes that include a segment on olive oil, which will give you an understanding of its importance in Puglian cuisine.

You'll develop a grasp of Puglia's olive oil legacy and how this precious liquid improves the region's culinary delights by delving into the world of olive oil tasting. This encounter will broaden your palate and strengthen your connection to Puglia's culinary culture.

4.2.3 Cooking Workshops

Cooking workshops in Puglia provide an intensive and hands-on method to learn about the region's culinary traditions. These seminars offer a unique opportunity to learn from professional chefs and understand the secrets behind Puglia's most beloved dishes, from kneading dough to perfecting native recipes.

Experience with a Cooking Class:

1. Local products: Begin your culinary session by experimenting with fresh local ingredients. Visit markets, farms, or local shops to get produce, cheeses, meats, and other ingredients that go into Puglian cuisine.

2. ancient Recipes: Learn how to cook famous Puglian dishes using ancient recipes handed down through generations under the supervision of skilled chefs. Some examples are orecchiette pasta, taralli, and frisella.

3. Roll up your sleeves and get your hands dirty in the kitchen. Knead dough, chop veggies, and stir sauces as you actively engage in the preparation of the food.

4. Techniques and Tips: Learn essential cooking techniques unique to Puglian cuisine. Learn the delicate balance of seasoning and the timing required for each stage in making great orecchiette.

5. Wine Pairing: Wine pairing skills are included in many cooking classes in Puglia. Learn how to compliment your works with local wines, increasing the flavors and boosting the overall eating experience.

6. Chefs frequently give anecdotes, cultural insights, and historical context related to the meals while you prepare. These tales help us better grasp Puglia's culinary tradition.

7. Dining Together: After you've finished cooking, gather around the table with your fellow participants to enjoy the results of your labor. Share your stories, taste your creations, and become immersed in the conviviality of Puglian dining culture.

Cooking School Locations:

A Cooking Day in Lecce: This Lecce cooking school offers hands-on training in a variety of Puglian dishes, from pasta making to dessert preparation.

Masseria Il Frantoio: This quaint masseria near Ostuni provides cooking classes centered on traditional Puglian recipes made with farm-fresh ingredients.

Apulia culinary Class: Located in the countryside near Alberobello, this culinary school provides a rustic atmosphere for an authentic Puglian cooking experience.

La Cucina del Gusto: In Bari, you can take classes at La Cucina del Gusto to learn about the city's culinary traditions and enjoy a delicious lunch.

Otranto Cooking Experience: Immerse yourself in the culinary world of Otranto with hands-on cooking classes that highlight regional flavors and skills.

Cooking workshops in Polignano a Mare: Learn the secrets of Puglian cuisine with workshops that emphasize the connection between food, culture, and the land.

Booking a Puglia cooking lesson allows you to delve deeper into the region's culinary history. From preparing pasta to tasting the results of your effort, you'll create memories and abilities that will last far beyond your time in the kitchen.

A Puglian cooking class is more than simply a culinary instruction; it's an opportunity to connect with the region's history, interact with local ingredients, and bring the flavors of Puglia home to your own kitchen. These lessons are a meaningful and tasty opportunity to interact with the heart and spirit of Puglian food, whether you're a seasoned cook or a beginner.

4.3 Souvenirs and traditional crafts

4.3.1 Pottery and ceramics

Puglia's cultural heritage extends beyond its cuisine to include a strong ceramics and pottery tradition. Puglian ceramics are noted for their elaborate designs, brilliant colors, and cultural significance, and are rooted in centuries of craftsmanship. Exploring this art form allows you to bring a piece of Puglian heritage and ingenuity home with you.

Experience with ceramics and pottery:
1. Visit local pottery workshops to observe craftsmen in operation. Watch as the clay is carefully molded, shaped, painted, and fired to create exquisite ceramic sculptures.

2. Insight into Craftsmanship: Interact with the craftspeople to learn about their skills, the symbolism behind certain designs, and the role ceramics play in Puglian life.

3. Ceramics Variety: Discover a vast range of ceramics, from functional pieces such as plates, bowls, and vases to ornamental items such as tiles, figurines, and ornate ornaments.

4. Puglian ceramics frequently include unique designs, such as geometric patterns, floral themes, and representations of local landscapes, providing a genuine touch to your gift.

5. Hands-On Experience: Some workshops provide hands-on experiences where you can try your hand at making pottery while being guided by expert artisans.

6. Customization: Many workshops allow you to

personalize your pottery by selecting colors, patterns, and designs, resulting in a genuinely unique souvenir.

7. Learn about the historical significance of ceramics in Puglian culture, such as their role in daily life, religious rites, and architectural adornment.

Best Ways to Enjoy Puglian Ceramics

Visit renowned pottery workshops in cities such as Grottaglie, where you can browse galleries, meet artisans, and buy authentic pieces.

Local Markets: Look for pottery stalls at local markets where artisans sell their work. This allows for direct interaction with the creators.

Attend art festivals and craft fairs that include Puglian ceramics as well as other traditional crafts to compare styles and designs.

Visits to museums: Some museums in Puglia display historical ceramics, providing insights into the evolution of this art form and its cultural setting.

Visit pottery workshops as part of guided tours to gain a complete understanding of the trade.

Bringing home Puglian ceramics not only benefits local artists but also allows you to take home a piece of the region's artistic legacy. Puglian ceramics capture the beauty and skill of this enchanting region, whether it's a utilitarian piece for your house or a beautiful decoration.

4.3.2 Handwoven Fabrics

Introduction: Puglia's cultural tapestry includes handwoven textiles in addition to its food and ceramics. Puglian textiles, from carefully made fabrics to traditional outfits, reflect the region's history, workmanship, and aesthetic flair. Exploring these fabrics allows you to connect with Puglia's rich heritage while also purchasing one-of-a-kind and significant keepsakes.

Experience with Handwoven Textiles:

1. Traditional Weaving Workshops: Take a trip to a traditional weaving workshop, where trained artists use age-old techniques to transform raw materials into magnificent textiles.

2. Weaving Techniques: See how looms are set up, yarns are chosen, and intricate designs are woven, which are typically inspired by local landscapes and customs.

3. Textile Varieties: Discover a diverse assortment of handcrafted textiles such as tablecloths, linens, scarves, shawls, and even traditional costumes such as pagnotta and pizzo (lace).

4. Local Materials: Discover how locally derived materials such as cotton, linen, and wool are utilized in weaving and how they contribute to the textures and colors of the textiles.

5. Conversations with Weavers: Engage in conversations with weavers to learn about the

cultural significance of their work, the tales behind the designs, and the role of textiles in Puglian life.

6. Textile Craftsmanship Insight: Gain an understanding of the complexities of textile craftsmanship, from pattern selection to weaving techniques, as well as the passion necessary to create each piece.

7. Souvenirs: Select from a wide range of handmade fabrics that speak to you, each capturing the essence of Puglia's history and craftsmanship.

The Best Ways to Enjoy Puglian Handwoven Textiles:

Visit weaving workshops in towns like Martina Franca and Locorotondo, where you can see weavers at work and buy handmade wares.

Attend craft fairs and artisan markets that exhibit handwoven textiles, providing a broad assortment of works from various districts of Puglia.

Visits to museums: Some museums in Puglia offer exhibits on traditional textiles that provide insights into the historical and cultural context of these creations.

Cultural excursions: Participate in cultural excursions that include visits to textile studios, allowing you to immerse yourself in the world of Puglian textiles.

Custom Orders: Some craftsmen offer custom orders, allowing you to create a one-of-a-kind piece based on your specifications.

By bringing home Puglian handwoven textiles, you are not only purchasing a functional piece of art, but also conserving the tradition of skilled artisans. These textiles encapsulate the heart and soul of Puglia's textile traditions, allowing you to appreciate the region's cultural richness from the comfort of your own home.

4.3.3 Local Craftspeople

Introduction: The labor of local artisans who dedicate their abilities to maintaining traditional handicraft is intimately intertwined into Puglia's cultural character. Puglian artists make pieces that symbolize the region's heritage, ingenuity, and dedication to conserving centuries-old skills, from delicate lacework to complex woodwork.

Local Artists' Knowledge:

1. Visit the workshops of local artists to witness the magic of their hands at work. Take note of the rich details and the care that has gone into each creation.

2. trade Demonstrations: Many craftsmen provide live demonstrations of their trade, allowing you to observe the process from beginning to end and obtain a better understanding of their abilities.

3. Conversations with Artisans: Talk with artisans about their journey, the significance of their craft in

Puglian culture, and how they've adapted old techniques for current times.

4. Explore a variety of crafts such as wood carving, lace making, metallurgy, needlepoint, and more. Each craft has its own history and symbolism.

5. Custom Orders: Some craftsmen accept custom orders, allowing you to create a one-of-a-kind creation that is personalized to your preferences while capturing the essence of Puglia.

6. Local Markets & Boutiques: Visit markets, boutiques, and craft shows to see the work of local artisans. These establishments frequently curate a variety of handcrafted objects that demonstrate the breadth of Puglian workmanship.

7. Cultural Context: Discover the cultural context of each craft, from traditional purposes to the part they play in Puglian celebrations and daily life.

The Best Ways to Discover Puglian Artisans:

Artisan Trails: In some parts of Puglia, there are official artisan trails that lead to workshops and studios where you can meet artisans and purchase their goods.

Craft fairs and artist markets bring together a number of local craftspeople under one roof, allowing you to experience a variety of crafts.

Guided Tours: Take part in guided tours that include visits to artisan workshops, which provide insights into various crafts and their historical significance.

Online Platforms: Look into online platforms that connect you with Puglian craftsmen, allowing you to purchase their work and help them support their families.

Cultural Centers and Museums: Cultural centers and museums frequently offer exhibitions exhibiting the work of local artisans, providing you with a thorough grasp of their trade.

By interacting with Puglian craftsmen, you are not only purchasing handcrafted items but also assisting in the preservation of traditional workmanship. These works capture the essence of Puglia's cultural heritage and provide a visible link to the region's artistic history.

25 Exciting Activities in Puglia

5.1 Discover Alberobello's Trulli

A Journey Into Puglia's Unique Architecture. Alberobello is a UNESCO World Heritage Site known for its lovely trulli, ancient stone houses with characteristic conical roofs. These prominent structures bear witness to Puglia's architectural legacy and provide insight into the region's history and culture. Exploring the trulli is a must-do activity for any visitor to Puglia.

What You Should Do

Wander Through Trulli Districts: Take a leisurely stroll through the Rione Monti and Aia Piccola districts, which are lined with groupings of trulli. These well-preserved neighborhoods offer a genuine ambience as well as several photo opportunities.

Explore Trullo Sovrano, a two-story trullo that also serves as a museum. Inside, you'll find historical relics, furnishings, and insights into trullo residents' daily lives.

Souvenirs: Browse local businesses within trulli regions for one-of-a-kind souvenirs such as handcrafted ceramics, local crafts, and traditional Puglian items.

Dine in a Trattoria: Experience authentic Puglian cuisine by dining in a trulli-turned-trattoria. Enjoy local foods and wines while immersed in the building's rustic charm.

The best way to experience and discover

Join a guided walking tour led by educated locals who can give historical nuggets and cultural anecdotes about the trulli and their significance.

Arrive early in the morning to avoid crowds and to capture the peaceful beauty of the trulli districts.

Interaction with Locals: Interact with locals to learn about their trulli lives and obtain insights into the history and evolution of these unique constructions.

How to Get There

Alberobello is located roughly 70 kilometers from Bari. You can get to Alberobello by train or bus from Bari.

From Brindisi: You can also take a rail or bus to Alberobello from Brindisi.

By Car: Renting a car allows users greater freedom and convenience when exploring the surrounding areas.

Exploring Alberobello's trulli brings you to a world of whimsical architecture and cultural riches. You'll obtain a profound appreciation for the distinctiveness of Puglia's trulli and their significance in the region's identity by strolling through the historic neighborhoods, seeing the museum, and mingling with people.

5.2 Wandering around Ostuni's White-Washed Streets

Discovering the Charms of the "White City". Ostuni, sometimes known as the "White City" because of its brilliant white-washed buildings, is a mesmerizing destination that embodies Puglian architecture and culture. It's like walking into a captivating white and blue artwork as you wander through its convoluted alleyways.

What You Should Do

Explore the Historic core: Take a self-guided walking tour of the historic core of Ostuni, snaking through narrow alleyways, secret squares, and ancient archways.

Explore the majestic Ostuni Cathedral (Cattedrale di Ostuni), with its gorgeous façade and stunning interior. Take in the rose window and architectural details.

Climb to the highest point in Ostuni to access picturesque vantage points with panoramic views of the Adriatic Sea, nearby farms, and the sea of white roofs.

Explore local boutiques and artist shops for one-of-a-kind Puglian crafts, ceramics, textiles, and more. Ostuni is an excellent spot to buy genuine souvenirs.

The best way to experience and discover

Sunset Stroll: Take a stroll through the streets of Ostuni at sunset, when the white walls radiate warmth and the town takes on a lovely glow.

Keep your camera handy to capture the play of light and shadow on the white facades, creating spectacular photo compositions.

Local Gastronomy: Sample traditional Puglian meals in the delightful setting of local restaurants that line the streets.

How to Get There:
Ostuni is around 100 kilometers from Bari. Ostuni can be reached by train, bus, or car. The train excursion provides scenic views of the Puglian countryside.

From Brindisi: The trip to Ostuni is around 40 kilometers long and may be completed by train, bus, or car.

A stroll through Ostuni's white-washed streets is an immersive experience that reveals the town's architectural grandeur, historical significance, and enchanting beauty. Ostuni welcomes you to experience its distinct charms, whether you're visiting its historic landmarks, enjoying stunning views, or simply soaking in the charm of its lanes.

5.3 Discover Matera's Ancient Cave City

Uncovering History in the Heart of Basilicata

Matera, in the nearby area of Basilicata, is an intriguing destination noted for its historic cave homes and distinctive urban setting. Matera's millennia-old history provides a voyage back in time as well as a profound link to Italy's cultural legacy.

What You Should Do

Wander through the Sassi di Matera, Matera's ancient cave houses and stone-carved settlements. Explore the troglodyte construction that dates back to antiquity.

Explore the fascinating cave churches of Matera, which are filled with paintings, rock-cut altars, and holy art. The rupestrian churches shed light on the region's spiritual history.

MUSMA - Museum of Contemporary Sculpture: Explore an underground complex that houses an art museum unlike any other. MUSMA displays contemporary sculptures in an environment that effortlessly integrates modern art and ancient architecture.

Piazza Vittorio Veneto: Unwind in Piazza Vittorio Veneto, a key square with panoramic views of the Sassi and a hub for cafés, restaurants, and cultural activities.

The best way to experience and discover:
Guided Tours: Take part in guided tours that provide historical context and fascinating stories about Matera's transformation from cave city to vibrant modern attraction.

Sunrise or Sunset: Visit the Sassi at sunrise or sunset to see how light and shade interact to accentuate the dramatic grandeur of the cave houses.

Cultural Immersion: Interact with locals, possibly by joining a cooking class or workshop, to learn about Matera's traditional crafts, cuisine, and way of life.

How to Get There:
Matera is around 65 kilometers away from Bari. You can get from Bari to Matera via train or bus. The ride provides stunning views of the countryside.

Conclusion: Matera's ancient cave city is a tribute to human inventiveness and the continuity of life over time. Exploring the Sassi, cave churches, and modern art among this breathtaking setting allows you to understand Matera's rich history and culture. The trek to Matera is a journey into the past that is both profound and transformative.

4. Visit the Castel del Monte - Exploring Puglia's Architectural Wonders

Castel del Monte, a UNESCO World Heritage site, is a unique architectural jewel in Puglia. Its unusual octagonal shape, strategic location, and interesting history make it a must-see attraction that captivates both travelers and history buffs.

What You Should Do
Admire the Architecture: Take in the distinctive octagonal architecture of Castel del Monte, which is distinguished by its harmonious proportions and mix of architectural styles.

Explore the Castle's Interior: Enter the castle and explore its rooms, halls, and chambers. Examine the rich intricacies in the stone-carved ornaments and architectural features.

Ascend the castle's towers to enjoy stunning panoramic views of the surrounding area, which includes the Apulian countryside and the Adriatic Sea.

Visit the interpretative center on the castle grounds to learn about the history, purpose, and symbolism behind Castel del Monte's construction.

The best way to experience and discover:
Guided Tours: Participate in guided tours offered by trained professionals who can provide historical context and architectural insights, furthering your understanding of the castle.

Audio Guides: Many locations have audio guides that allow you to explore the castle at your own pace, allowing you to delve into its history at your leisure.

How to Get There
Castel del Monte is around 60 kilometers from Bari. It is accessible by automobile or public transit, including as buses running between Bari and Andria.

Castel del Monte is a tribute to medieval architecture's grandeur as well as the cultural significance it possesses in Puglian history. By visiting this well-known UNESCO realm Heritage site, you will enter a realm where history, design, and symbolism intersect, providing a peek into the past and a link to Puglia's enduring attraction.

5. Attend a Traditional Pizzica Dance Festival to immerse yourself in the vibrant folk culture of Puglia.

Introduction: The rhythmic pulses of the Pizzica dance bring Puglia's folk culture to life. Attending a Pizzica dance festival provides an exciting opportunity to participate with the region's vibrant culture, music, and dance, as well as to connect with the local community.

What You Should Do
Watch the Pizzica dance shows, which are distinguished by dynamic moves, strong footwork, and intriguing music. Immerse yourself in the contagious rhythm and upbeat atmosphere.

Join the Dance: Don't be afraid to get on the dance floor and try your hand (or feet) at the Pizzica. Locals are frequently ready to share their dance moves and create a festive mood.

Enjoy the sounds of traditional Puglian music, such as accordion, tambourines, and other folk instruments that accompany the Pizzica dance.

Pizzica festivals frequently feature local craft stalls where you may explore and purchase traditional crafts, textiles, and artisanal goods.

The best way to experience and discover:
Participation in Festivals: Plan your trip around Pizzica dance festivals, which typically take place throughout the summer months. Keep an eye out for announcements about upcoming festivals and their scheduling.

Interaction with Locals: During the event, interact with locals to learn about the significance of Pizzica dance, its cultural roots, and its part in Puglian celebrations.

How to Get There
Pizzica celebrations are conducted in several cities and villages throughout Puglia. Look for announcements and marketing to locate festivals that correspond to your travel plans.

Attending a Pizzica dance festival allows you to experience Puglia's rich folk culture firsthand, enjoying the vivid beat, intriguing dances, and enthusiastic spirit of the region. By taking part in this celebration event, you will strengthen your ties to the local community and create lasting memories of your journey across Puglia's cultural landscape.

6. Take a Boat Tour Through the Grotta della Poesia Sea Caves

A Nautical Adventure in Puglia

Introduction: The coast of Puglia is dotted with natural treasures, and the Grotta della Poesia sea caverns are among the most enthralling. A boat tour of these caves provides a unique perspective on the region's marine beauty and geological wonders.

What You Should Do

Admire the Rock Formations: Cruise across the turquoise waves, passing by the Puglian coast's spectacular rock formations and limestone cliffs.

Enter the Grotta della Poesia: Venture into the Grotta della Poesia, a captivating and evocative sea cave. Its crystal-clear seas beckon you to go swimming or snorkeling.

Discover Hidden Coves: Discover hidden coves and isolated beaches accessible only by boat, allowing you to appreciate the peace and quiet of the coastline away from the masses.

Photograph the grandeur of the sea caves and their surroundings to create lasting memories of this stunning natural wonder.

The best way to experience and discover:
Join guided boat tours that traverse the Grotta della Poesia and its surrounds, assuring safety and providing insights into the geological treasures.

Swimming and Snorkeling: If permitted, take advantage of the opportunity to swim or snorkel in the Grotta della Poesia's crystal-clear waters. The experience is both exhilarating and rejuvenating.

How to Get There
Local travel firms in coastal communities such as Roca Vecchia typically offer boat journeys to the Grotta della Poesia. Look for reputable operators and make reservations ahead of time.

Conclusion: A boat excursion along the Grotta della Poesia sea caves provides a glimpse into the coastal allure of Puglia, displaying the harmonic interplay of sea and rock formations. Immersing yourself in Puglia's seaside beauty will allow you to uncover the enchantment of these hidden treasures and create unforgettable experiences.

7. Torre Lapillo's Serene Beaches - A Coastal Paradise with Crystal-Clear Waters

Torre Lapillo's magnificent shoreline and clear

oceans provide an excellent location for beach enthusiasts seeking relaxation and natural beauty. This Puglian destination has lovely sandy shores that beckon you to relax, swim, and soak up the sun.

What You Should Do

Swim in Crystal-pure Waters: Cool off in the refreshing and amazingly pure waters that characterise Torre Lapillo's beaches. Swimming and wading are made more enjoyable by the calm sea.

Relaxation and sunbathing: Lie back on the beautiful sandy beaches and soak up the Mediterranean sun. The peaceful ambiance and mild sea wind provide the ideal setting for relaxation.

Beach Activities: Play beach volleyball, paddleboard, or simply build sandcastles with friends and family.

Explore undersea: If you enjoy snorkeling, explore the undersea environment, which is filled with marine life, colorful fish, and even unusual underwater rock formations.

The best way to experience and discover:
Visit Torre Lapillo early in the morning to enjoy the beaches before they become crowded. This is an excellent opportunity to capture tranquil moments

and gorgeous photographs.

Beachside Dining: Many beaches have beachside cafés and restaurants where you may eat local seafood while looking out at the sea.

How to Get There

Public Transportation: To go to Torre Lapillo, take a bus from Lecce or another neighboring town. Make sure to check the bus route ahead of time.

Car Rental: Renting a car allows you to go to Torre Lapillo more easily and explore other surrounding sights.

Conclusion: Torre Lapillo's quiet beaches are ideal for people seeking natural beauty, tranquility, and the delight of the sea. This seaside paradise encourages you to absorb the spirit of Puglia's coastal charm, whether you're enjoying the water, sunbathing, or simply admiring the coastal panorama.

8. Hike the Gargano National Park's Coastal Path - Discovering Nature's Masterpiece

Introduction: Gargano National Park, a beautiful coastal paradise, allows hikers to go on a trip across different landscapes that harmoniously combine sea and land. The park's seaside route leads to breathtaking views, rare flora and fauna, and a deep connection with nature.

What You Should Do

The Coastal Scenic Trail winds through the Gargano National Park, providing panoramic views of the Adriatic Sea, stunning cliffs, and secret bays.

Explore Diverse Landscapes: Travel through a variety of landscapes, including lush forests, rugged cliffs, sandy beaches, and lovely coastal villages.

Discover uncommon Flora and Fauna: Keep an eye out for the park's unique flora and fauna, which includes uncommon plants, bird species, and other wildlife.

Relaxation and photography: Capture the spectacular coastline views and natural beauty as you take a break to relax and refresh in nature's embrace.

The best way to experience and discover:
Guided treks: Join guided treks conducted by local experts to learn about the park's natural beauty, history, and environmental significance.

Wear appropriate hiking shoes, bring plenty of

water and food, and make sure you have sun protection and a trail guide.

How to Get There

By automobile: The Gargano National Park is accessible by automobile from local towns and cities. Prepare by researching trailheads and parking options.

Public Transportation: Public transportation is accessible in several locations of the park. Examine the nearby bus lines that link to the park.

Hiking along Gargano National Park's coastal path allows you to immerse yourself in the region's unspoilt beauty and different sceneries. As you walk the trail, you'll develop a stronger connection with nature and obtain a better understanding of the diverse ecosystems that make this park a true natural masterpiece in the heart of Puglia.

9. Explore the Frantoio Ipogeo's Underground Olive Oil Mills - Unveiling Ancient Olive Oil Traditions

Puglia has a rich olive oil legacy, and the Frantoio Ipogeo provides an intriguing peek into this practice by allowing visitors to explore ancient underground olive oil mills. Explore the history of olive oil production to discover the brilliance of the past.

What You Should Do

Visit the Underground Mills: Take a guided tour of the network of underground olive oil mills. Learn about the various procedures involved in the manufacturing of olive oil.

Observe Historical equipment: See the historic equipment and machinery that were used in centuries past for crushing, pressing, and extracting olive oil.

Learn About Olive Oil Production: Discover the entire process of producing olive oil, from harvesting the olives to bottling the finished product.

Fresh Olive Oil Tasting: Many trips include an olive oil tasting session where you can sample the various varieties made by the frantoio.

The best way to experience and discover:
Guided Tours: Join one of the Frantoio Ipogeo's guided tours to properly understand the historical significance and sophisticated art of olive oil production.

Local Experts: Meet with qualified guides who can explain the history and culture of olive oil in Puglia.

How to Get There

The Frantoio Ipogeo is located in the Salento region of Italy. In ahead, look up the actual address and business hours.

Car Rental: Renting a car allows you to get to the Frantoio Ipogeo and other surrounding attractions with ease and flexibility.

Exploring the underground olive oil mills at the Frantoio Ipogeo transports you back in time to learn about the region's deep ties to olive oil production. You'll develop a great respect for the craft, history, and relevance of olive oil in Puglia's culture and culinary landscape by delving into this age-old tradition.

10. Participate in a Cooking Class to Learn Traditional Puglian Dishes - Savoring the Region's Flavors

Puglia's culinary tradition is an important part of its culture, and what better way to learn about it than to take a cooking class? Immerse yourself in the art of Puglian cooking, from the selection of fresh ingredients to the creation of traditional meals handed down through generations.

What You Should Do

Hands-On Cooking Experience: Get your hands dirty and actively participate in the production of Puglian cuisine. Learn essential skills like preparing fresh pasta and mastering the art of taste balancing.

Traditional Recipes: Try traditional Puglian cuisine including orecchiette pasta, focaccia, burrata cheese, and seafood dishes. Learn the secrets of each dish's flavor.

Visits to Local Markets: Some cooking sessions include visits to local markets, where you'll select fresh ingredients while engaging with merchants and learning about Puglian food culture.

Savor Your Creations: After you've finished cooking, take a seat and enjoy the results of your labor. Indulge in a substantial supper of your own creations, accompanied by local wines.

The best way to experience and discover:
skilled Chefs: Choose workshops taught by skilled

chefs or local home cooks who may offer personalized advise and share anecdotes about Puglian culinary traditions.

Small Group lessons: Participate in small group lessons for a more intimate and dynamic experience that allows you to receive individualized treatment.

How to Get There

Booking: Do your research and book culinary classes ahead of time to ensure availability during your travel dates.

Finally, taking a cooking lesson in Puglia is a sensory experience that allows you to taste, touch, and feel the essence of the region's cuisine. By learning to make classic Puglian dishes, you will not only improve your culinary skills, but you will also develop a greater knowledge of the cultural significance of food in Puglian life.

11. Discover Otranto's Medieval Town - Immerse Yourself in History and Art

Otranto, a lovely medieval village on the Puglian coast, is a historical and cultural treasure trove. Otranto invites you to journey back in time and enjoy its rich history, from its charming alleyways to the stunning mosaic church floor.

What You Should Do

Explore the Historic Center: Stroll through Otranto's small alleyways and cobblestone streets, where centuries-old architecture and quaint buildings generate a sense of nostalgia.

Visit the Otranto Cathedral (Basilica Cattedrale di Santa Maria Annunziata), which is noted for its magnificent mosaic floor depicting elaborate religious and allegorical figures.

Discover the Aragonese Castle: Visit Otranto's Aragonese Castle, which overlooks the sea and provides panoramic views of the coastline. The castle also houses a museum with historical artifacts.

Relax by the Sea: Take a leisurely stroll down Otranto's promenade, admiring the sights of the crystal-clear waters and possibly relaxing on the sandy beaches.

The best way to experience and discover:
Guided Tours: Join one of Otranto's guided walking tours to learn about its history, architecture, and cultural significance.

Audio tours: Some attractions have audio tours that provide detailed commentary while you visit the attractions at your own speed.

How to Get There

Public Transportation: From many cities in Puglia, Otranto is accessible by train, bus, or vehicle. The journey provides stunning views of the region's surroundings.

Otranto offers an enthralling blend of history, art, and seashore beauty. Exploring its medieval streets, seeing the cathedral's exquisite mosaic floor, and taking in the panoramic views from the castle transport you to another age. Immersing yourself in Otranto's cultural tapestry will leave you with a deep appreciation for the town's place in Puglia's rich historical narrative.

12. A Scenic Cycling Adventure through the Picturesque Countryside of the Itria Valley

The Itria Valley, with its rolling hills, beautiful towns, and distinctive trulli, is a cyclist's paradise. Exploring this picturesque landscape on two wheels provides an intimate connection with the Puglian countryside as well as the opportunity to find hidden jewels along the road.

What You Should Do

Cycle through the classic trulli settlements, such as Alberobello and Locorotondo. Admire the unique architecture and enjoy the rustic charm of these communities.

Enjoy Scenic Routes: There are numerous bicycle routes that pass past olive groves, vineyards, and wildflower fields. Take in the breathtaking valley panoramas.

Visit rural farms to learn about traditional farming practices, olive oil production, and wine-making skills.

Explore the Almond Fields: Depending on the season, you may be able to cycle through almond fields that are in full bloom, creating a visually fascinating experience.

The best way to experience and discover:
Bike Rentals: Bicycles can be rented from local stores or guided tour companies that offer riding packages.

Guided excursions: Choose guided cycling excursions lead by professionals who know the region's routes, history, and cultural features.

How to Get There:
Base point: To begin your cycling tour, choose a base point in the Itria Valley, such as Alberobello or Martina Franca.

Cycling across the Itria Valley is an exhilarating way to explore the core of Puglia's landscape. You'll develop a sensory connection to the region's landscapes, history, and rural customs as you pedal through trulli villages, appreciate the tranquillity of olive orchards, and soak in the natural splendor.

13. Visit Gallipoli's Historic Town - A Journey Through Time and Coastal Beauty

Gallipoli, a coastal town with a rich history and enchanting environment, invites visitors to explore its picturesque old town and revel in the beauty of its beaches. This location elegantly blends historical legacy with beach allure.

What You Should Do

Explore the Old Town: Take a stroll around Gallipoli's old town, a maze of narrow streets, historic churches, and centuries-old structures. Admire the sea-protection walls that surround the town.

Explore the Cathedral of Saint Agatha (Cattedrale di Sant'Agata), a magnificent structure decorated with intricate embellishments and artwork.

Enjoy the magnificent sandy beaches of Gallipoli, where you may relax in the sun, swim in the turquoise waves, and unwind by the sea.

Explore Gallipoli Castle: Gallipoli Castle is a well-known fortress with panoramic views of the sea and town. The castle also houses the Museum of the Sea and Civilizations of Gallipoli.

The best way to experience and discover:
Guided Walking Tours: Participate in guided walking tours of Gallipoli's ancient town to learn about its history, architectural treasures, and cultural significance.

Beach Time: Set aside some time to enjoy the beaches, whether you're looking for relaxation or water-based activities.

How to Get There

Gallipoli is accessible by train, bus, or car from many places around Puglia. The coastal train journey provides spectacular sights.

Finally, Gallipoli invites you to explore its storied past and seaside beauty. From the cobblestone alleyways of the old town to the tempting beaches, this destination provides a mix of historical exploration and seaside relaxation. You'll leave Gallipoli with memories that capture the spirit of this enchanting town if you immerse yourself in its history and appreciate its natural beauty.

14. Discover the Charm of Weekly Markets - Martina Franca Market and More

Weekly markets in Puglia are dynamic hubs of local culture, giving a lively environment, fresh produce, artisan products, and the opportunity to engage with people. The Martina Franca market, for example, provides an enthralling peek into the region's daily life and traditions.

What You Should Do

Wander through the lively market stalls filled with fresh fruits and vegetables, cheeses, cured meats, and local specialties. Engage merchants and look for localized products.

Discover Handcrafted things: Browse handmade

crafts, fabrics, ceramics, and other one-of-a-kind things that highlight Puglia's artistic legacy.

Savor Street Food: From crispy taralli and savory panzerotti to sweet pasticciotti, indulge in street food selections. These regional delicacies offer a taste of Puglian cuisine.

Immerse yourself in the market's bustling environment, where locals gather to mingle, shop, and celebrate the region's gastronomic and artisanal practices.

The best way to experience and discover:
Arrive early to catch the market at its busiest and to receive the best assortment of fresh vegetables and items.

Engage with Locals: Start conversations with sellers to learn about their products, the culinary history of the region, and local customs.

How to Get There

Market Days: Find out the specific days and times of the Martina Franca market, as well as any other weekly markets you want to visit.

Visiting Puglia's weekly markets, particularly the Martina Franca market, provides a dynamic and real immersion into the region's native life and customs. You'll acquire insights into the core of Puglia's communal spirit and cultural wealth by interacting with sellers, sampling regional delights, and discovering handcrafted treasures.

15. Explore Matera's Historic Center's Unique "Sassi" Architecture - A Journey into Ancient Dwellings

Matera's "Sassi," a complex of ancient cave houses and rock-cut buildings, is a UNESCO World Heritage site that invites you to take a step back in time and witness an unrivaled architectural masterpiece. This historic district has a one-of-a-kind scenery that is both engaging and evocative.

What You Should Do

Wander through Sasso Caveoso and Sasso Barisano: Discover the Sassi's two main regions, Sasso Caveoso and Sasso Barisano. Explore narrow passageways, stone-carved dwellings, and antique churches.

Visit Cave homes: Immerse yourself in the past by entering the cave homes and learning more about the everyday lives and creativity of the people who once called these caves home.

Visit Casa Grotta di Vico Solitario, a preserved cave home that provides insight into former lifestyles, furniture, and traditions.

Explore historic rock churches that are carved straight into the rock walls and are embellished with frescoes and religious art.

The best way to experience and discover

Guided Tours: Join guided tours that provide historical context, architectural insights, and stories about the evolution of the Sassi over time.

dusk and sunrise: Take a walk through the Sassi at sunrise or dusk to see the mellow light cast fascinating shadows on the rock formations and structures.

How to Get There

Guided trips: Guided trips to the Sassi are frequently available from local towns. Consider taking a tour to gain a complete understanding of the location.

Conclusion: Exploring Matera's old center's Sassi architecture is a journey into a world of ancient wonders and human creativity. You'll gain a profound appreciation of Matera's unique legacy and its significance as a UNESCO World legacy site as you walk the streets, explore cave dwellings, and uncover the artistry of rock-cut architecture.

16. Take a Wine Tour through the Vineyards of Salento - A Culinary and Viticultural Odyssey

The Salento region is a wine lover's paradise, and a wine tour through its magnificent vineyards provides an immersive immersion into the world of agriculture. Explore the craft of winemaking, sample the famous Primitivo wine, and experience the flavors that define the region.

What You Should Do

Visits to Vineyards: Take guided tours of local vineyards to learn about the winemaking process, from grape production to fermentation and aging.

Taste Primitivo Wine: Indulge in wine tastings, particularly of Salento's famous Primitivo wine, which is known for its robust and rich flavor.

Meet Winemakers: Interact with winemakers and specialists who share their love for viticulture and provide insights into the region's distinct terroir and practices.

Wine and Food Pairing: Indulge in wine and food pairing experiences that demonstrate the harmonious marriage of Primitivo wine with regional cuisine.

The best way to experience and discover:
Join guided wine tours organized by local wineries or tour providers. These tours provide a comprehensive overview of the winemaking process as well as the region's vinicultural heritage.

Designated Driver: If you intend to taste several wines, plan for transportation or designate a driver.

How to Get There:
Booking: Research and book wine excursions ahead of time because they may have limited availability, especially during high seasons.

A wine walk through the vineyards of Salento allows you to taste the region's nuances, both in its wines and in its culture. Engaging with winemakers, drinking the valued Primitivo wine, and visiting the stunning surroundings will increase your appreciation for the art of winemaking and the sensory delights that the Salento region has to offer.

17. Visit Polignano a Mare, a cliffside gem on the Adriatic coast.

Polignano a Mare, perched precipitously on cliffs overlooking the Adriatic Sea, is a postcard-perfect seaside town that entices visitors with its spectacular views, ancient charm, and active culture. A visit to this attractive location delivers natural beauty as well as cultural exploration.

What You Should Do:
Stroll around the famed Lama Monachile Beach, which is surrounded by cliffs and has crystal-clear seas. It's a great place to unwind, take in the landscape, and take photos.

Explore the old Center: Take a stroll through the old center of Polignano a Mare, admiring the whitewashed buildings, traditional architecture, and bright flowers.

Admire the Sea Views: Take in the breathtaking panoramic sea views from the cliffside viewpoints, which capture the magnificence of the Adriatic coastline.

Visit Domenico Modugno's Statue: Pay your respects to the town's famous son, Domenico Modugno, by paying a visit to his statue. "Volare" by Modugno became a worldwide smash.

The best way to experience and discover:
Sunset Views: Come in the late afternoon to witness

the magic of the sunset as it casts warm hues over the cliffs and water.

Explore at Your Own Pace: Take your time walking throughout town, discovering secret corners and soaking in the atmosphere.

How to Get There:
Polignano a Mare is accessible by train or bus from neighboring towns. The train station is a short walk from the town center.

Polignano a Mare is a visual treat with its majestic cliffs, turquoise seas, and lovely streets. You'll explore the unique character and allure of this coastal gem by visiting its beach, historic center, and local treasures. Polignano a Mare will make an everlasting impact on your Puglia journey, whether you're looking for pleasure, adventure, or cultural enrichment.

18. A Culinary Journey into Liquid Gold: Traditional Olive Oil Tasting at a Local Masseria
Introduction: Puglia's reputation as an olive oil haven is well-deserved, and a visit to a local masseria (farmhouse) offers a genuine opportunity to immerse oneself in the world of olive oil production. Learn about the nuances of olive oil, from farming to tasting, by engaging your senses and palate.

What You Should Do:
Start with a guided tour of the masseria, where you'll see the olive orchards and the processes involved in creating high-quality olive oil.

Learn About Olive kinds: Explore the various olive kinds grown in the region, each of which contributes distinct flavors and smells to the finished oil.

Olive Oil Tasting: Attend an expert-led olive oil tasting workshop. Learn how to recognize the subtleties of olive oil, such as its color, scent, taste, and texture.

Pairings and Usage Tips: Learn how to pair olive oil with food and how to use olive oil in your culinary ventures.

The best way to experience and discover:
Reservations: Many masserias provide guided tours and tastings upon request. To ensure availability, make reservations in advance.

Engage with professionals: Have a dialogue with the professionals who are leading the tasting, and ask questions to gain a better knowledge.

How to Get There:
Look for masserias in the neighborhood that offer

olive oil tastings and tours. Consider your options for getting to the masseria.

Finally, an olive oil tasting at a local masseria is an opportunity to delve deeply into the world of this prized liquid gold. You'll not only gain appreciation for Puglia's olive oil legacy but also a fresh understanding of the art and science behind this key element in Mediterranean cuisine by engaging your senses, learning about olive oil production, and experiencing the varied flavors.

19. Discover Cisternino's Hidden Gem - A Journey Through Enchanting Alleyways
Cisternino, located in the heart of the Itria Valley, is a hidden gem distinguished by its convoluted lanes, exquisite architecture, and timeless beauty. This little village invites visitors to venture off the beaten path and explore its charming streets.

What You Should Do:
Stroll through Cisternino's Historic Center: Take a leisurely stroll through the historic center, where you'll encounter whitewashed buildings, stone arches, and cobblestone streets.

Admire Trulli Architecture: Explore trulli, classic stone cottages with conical roofs spread across the village. These one-of-a-kind constructions are representative of the area.

Spend time at Piazza Vittorio Emanuele, the town's principal center, where you can relax at cafes, eat local food, and soak up the vibrant ambiance.

Wander through hidden courtyards and passageways, which are often decked with flowers and potted plants, creating a charming environment.

The best way to experience and discover:
Allow yourself to become lost in the maze of alleyways, as this is where the true character of the town emerges.

Local Cuisine: For a true gastronomic experience, savor local cuisine and flavors at the town's trattorias and cafes.

How to Get There:
Cisternino is easily accessible by train or bus from neighboring towns. Check schedules and links ahead of time.

Cisternino is an invitation to enter a world of peaceful charm and hidden beauty. You'll be fascinated by its genuineness and timeless appeal as you explore its winding lanes, uncover trulli, and absorb the town's tranquil environment. This hidden gem provides a look into the essence of Puglia, leaving you with unforgettable recollections.

20. Explore the Egnazia Archaeological Site - A Journey Through Millennia of History

Egnazia, an archaeological site rich in historical layers, provides an enthralling voyage through time. This historic settlement has remnants from several periods, providing insights into the region's past and the civilizations that formerly thrived here.

What You Should Do:

Explore the well-preserved Roman ruins, which include a marketplace, hot baths, and the remains of Roman palaces that once graced the landscape.

Learn about the Messapian culture through objects such as pottery, jewelry, and tools displayed in the on-site archaeological museum.

Ascend to the Acropolis, a fortified hilltop region with ruins from several ages that provide panoramic views of the surrounding environment.

Explore Byzantine Remnants: See Byzantine-era structures such as a basilica and a necropolis, which provide insight into the town's growth over time.

The best way to experience and discover:

Guided Tours: Join one of the archaeological site's guided tours to get historical context and insights into the significance of the ruins.

Museum journey: Begin your journey with the on-site archaeological museum, where you may learn more about the ruins.

How to Get There:
Egnazia is located close to Fasano. Plan your trip and transportation to the place carefully.

Exploring the ancient site of Egnazia is a fascinating journey through time and space. You'll obtain a greater knowledge of the layers of history that have molded the area by immersing yourself in the ruins, antiquities, and historical vestiges. Egnazia is a tribute to Puglia's eternal legacy, encouraging visitors to embark on an archaeological trip through the years.

21. Attend a local music or folklore festival and immerse yourself in the rhythms of Puglian culture.
Introduction: Music and folklore events bring Puglia's cultural liveliness to life. Attending these events allows you to experience the area's heart and soul, as traditional music, dances, and celebrations serve as a conduit for immersing oneself in Puglian culture.

What You Should Do:
Listen to traditional Puglian music, which is

commonly defined by instruments such as tambourines, accordions, and frame drums. The catchy melodies and rhythms are captivating.

Local Dances: See traditional dances like the Pizzica, a lively dance associated with the Taranta music genre. Participate or simply enjoy the exciting shows.

Taste Local Food: Many festivals feature traditional Puglian meals and street food, allowing you to sample regional flavors while immersing yourself in the joyous environment.

Participate in Celebrations: Join in on locals' celebrations, whether it's a patron saint feast, a harvest festival, or a cultural event that draws the community together.

The best way to experience and discover:
Festival Dates: Look up the dates of any local music or folklore festivals that will be taking place during your visit. These events are frequently held during holiday seasons.

Interact with people to learn about the festival's significance, traditions, and role in preserving Puglian culture.

How to Get There:

Local recommendations: Ask locals or your lodging hosts for recommendations on forthcoming music or folklore festivals.

Attending a local music or folklore festival in Puglia is an opportunity to become a part of the region's cultural fabric. Immersing yourself in the music, dance, and communal festivities will provide you with personal insights into customs that have been passed down through generations. These meetings are more than just events; they are portals into understanding the essence of Puglian identity and the spirit that preserves its cultural legacy.

22. Visit Locorotondo, a Circular Haven of Elegance.

Locorotondo, with its unusual circular structure and spotless white buildings, epitomizes Puglia's architectural beauty and cultural charm. This picturesque town encourages you to explore its streets, appreciate its elegance, and become immersed in its enchanting atmosphere.

What You Should Do:
Take a leisurely stroll through the old town of Locorotondo, admiring the well-preserved buildings with whitewashed walls and flower-adorned balconies.

Climb to the town's highest point for panoramic

views of the surrounding landscape, including the characteristic trulli roofs.

Explore the Church of St. George (Chiesa di San Giorgio), a jewel of Baroque architecture, and enjoy its magnificent interior.

Local Wines to Try: Locorotondo is well-known for its white wines. Visit local vineyards for wine samples and to learn about the region's viticultural culture.

The best way to experience and discover:
Morning Exploration: Begin your visit early in the morning to take advantage of the tranquil atmosphere and the greatest lighting for photography.

Local Cuisine: Savor classic trattorias, where you may sample Puglian flavors in a lovely environment.

How to Get There:
Locorotondo can be reached by train or bus from neighboring towns. Plan your trip and check timetables ahead of time.

The circular layout and ageless beauty of Locorotondo create an environment of tranquility and grace. You'll be enchanted by the town's beauty as you walk through its streets, admire its architectural splendor, and enjoy panoramic vistas. Locorotondo is more than simply a place; it's an experience that encapsulates Puglia's cultural and architectural history in a single, beautiful embrace.

23. Discover the Southern Beauty of Santa Maria di Leuca Lighthouse at Puglia's End.
The Santa Maria di Leuca lighthouse, located at the southernmost peninsula of Puglia, stands as a sentinel overlooking the Adriatic and Ionian Seas. This landmark monument, which represents the tip of Italy's heel and the meeting place of two oceans, provides a stunning vista.

What You Should Do:
Explore the Santa Maria di Leuca lighthouse, taking in its historic significance and architectural splendor. Climb to the peak for panoramic views.

Enjoy coastline vistas: From the lighthouse's high point, take in the magnificent coastline vistas. Take in the view of the azure waves stretching into the horizon.

Visit the Basilica of Santa Maria de Finibus Terrae, which is located close. This lovely chapel adds to the lighthouse's significance as a cultural and spiritual monument.

Take a stroll along the Promenade: Take a leisurely

stroll along the promenade that runs down the shoreline, taking in the fresh sea breeze and the picturesque sights.

The best way to experience and discover:
daybreak and sunset: The lighthouse's panoramic views are most appealing at daybreak and sunset. Visit during these hours for a truly amazing experience.

Bring your camera to capture the breathtaking vistas and the merging of two seas.

How to Get There:
Santa Maria di Leuca can be reached by vehicle or public transit. Plan your route and think about the best method to get to the southernmost point of Puglia.

The Santa Maria di Leuca lighthouse is more than just a navigational aid; it represents Puglia's connection to the sea and the grandeur of its surroundings. You'll make memories that mirror the charm of Puglia's southernmost edge by touring the lighthouse, taking in the coastline vistas, and savoring the splendor of this southern point.

24. Discover Monte Sant'Angelo, a Medieval Hilltop Town - A Spiritual and Historical Journey
Monte Sant'Angelo, perched on a mountaintop

overlooking the Adriatic Sea, is a medieval town rich in history and faith. Its historic sanctuary, a UNESCO World Heritage site, attracts pilgrims and tourists alike, who come to appreciate its profound significance and architectural beauty.

What You Should Do:
Visit the Sanctuary of Monte Sant'Angelo: Take a look around the Sanctuary of Monte Sant'Angelo, which is devoted to the archangel Michael. The cave shrine, where Michael is said to have appeared, is a place of pilgrimage and introspection.

Visit the Norman-Swabian Castle, an enormous fortress with panoramic views of the town, sea, and surrounding countryside.

Explore the Historic Center: Stroll through the ancient town's tiny streets, discovering its attractive architecture, modest shops, and local cafes.

Participate in religious services or join pilgrims in experiencing the spiritual environment of the sanctuary.

The best way to experience and discover:
Guided Tours: Consider participating in guided tours that provide historical and cultural context for the sanctuary and the significance of the town.

Quiet Contemplation: Take a minute to absorb the sanctuary's tranquillity and spirituality.

How to Get There:
Monte Sant'Angelo can be reached by vehicle or public transit. Plan your travel with the best route to this hilltop town in mind.

Monte Sant'Angelo is a one-of-a-kind combination of historical significance and spiritual resonance. Whether you come for the UNESCO-listed sanctuary, the medieval architecture, or the opportunity for peaceful reflection, your stay will be enhanced by the town's sense of timelessness and connection to centuries of pilgrimage and devotion. Enjoy the tranquillity of this hilltop refuge while learning about the layers of history that have shaped its identity.

25. Experience the Serenity and Tranquility of the Salina dei Monaci Salt Pans - a Natural Oasis of Flamingos

The Salina dei Monaci salt pans, located between the coastal villages of Margherita di Savoia and Barletta, provide a tranquil getaway into a world of natural beauty and avian wonders. This protected region is not only a home for migratory birds, but also a haven of peace for people seeking a one-of-a-kind connection with nature.

What You Should Do:
Observe Flamingos: Take in the sight of pink flamingos in their natural habitat, which are beautiful and attractive. These migratory birds offer a dash of color to the otherwise tranquil setting.

Capture the hypnotic landscapes of the salt pans, the reflections on the water's surface, and the magnificent presence of the flamingos with your camera.

Nature Walks: Take nature walks along the established trails to become immersed in the sights, sounds, and fragrances of the salt pans.

Relaxation: Find a peaceful place to rest and unwind, taking in the magnificent vistas and enjoying some privacy in nature.

The best way to experience and discover:
Early Mornings: The early morning hours are ideal for birdwatching and enjoying the peace and quiet of the salt pans.

Binoculars: Bring binoculars to keep a reasonable distance from the flamingos and other bird species.

How to Get There
The salt pans are easily accessible by car. Make plans to visit this natural retreat.

The Salina dei Monaci salt pans provide a look into nature's delicate equilibrium, where flamingos take sanctuary and peace reigns. Immersing yourself in the natural beauty of this place will lead you to a calm oasis where the sounds of birds and the stillness of the water form a symphony of tranquility. It's an invitation to slow down, connect with the natural world's cycles, and savor the beauty that flourishes in the Salina dei Monaci's simplicity.

26. Hike the Paths of Alta Murgia National Park - Panoramic Vistas Surrounded by Natural Beauty

Alta Murgia National Park, with its rolling hills, historic olive trees, and mountainous landscapes, is a trekking paradise for both nature lovers and adventurers. Exploring its routes provides you with magnificent vistas of this distinct and diverse landscape.

What You Should Do:
Choose a Hiking Trail: Choose a hiking trail that is appropriate for your ability level and interests. The length and intensity of the trails varies, providing

opportunities for both casual walkers and avid hikers.

Traverse across limestone plateaus, lush meadows, and rocky terrain, each showing a distinct aspect of the park's natural splendor.

Capture Vistas: Hike to viewpoints along the trails that offer panoramic views of the park's valleys, hills, and the Adriatic Sea.

Observation of fauna: Keep an eye out for the park's diverse fauna, which includes birds of prey, foxes, and wildflowers.

The best way to experience and discover

Guided Hikes: Take advantage of guided hiking trips offered by local specialists who can provide information about the park's vegetation, animals, and geological structures.

Pack essentials such as good boots, water, snacks, a map, and sun protection for a safe and enjoyable hiking adventure.

How to Get There

Alta Murgia National Park can be reached by

automobile or public transit. Investigate the optimal entry points based on your selected path.

Hiking the routes of Alta Murgia National Park is an invitation to connect with nature's majesty and the raw beauty of the region. You'll realize that every step is a trip into a diversified world of natural splendor as you explore its trails, climb to vistas, and take in the far-reaching views. Hiking routes in the park provide not only stunning vistas, but also an opportunity to reconnect with the peace and majesty of nature.

27. A Serene Equestrian Adventure on Horseback Through Olive Groves and Countryside

Exploring Puglia's stunning surroundings on horseback adds a touch of romance and a connection with nature. Riding through olive groves, rolling hills, and tiny towns provides a unique perspective, enabling you to take in the region's beauty at your own pace.

What You Should Do

Choose a Riding path: Select a horseback riding path that is appropriate for your level of experience and desired terrain. Consider options such as olive groves, countryside, and tourist attractions.

Spend Time Bonding with Your Horse: Before going on a ride, spend time bonding with your horse. Making friends with your horse increases the experience for both of you.

Enjoy the scenic vistas as you meander through olive fields, cross hills, and feel the soothing rhythm of your horse's pace.

Bring a camera to record the beauty of the countryside and the delight of your equestrian adventure.

The best way to experience and discover
Guided Tours: Choose guided horseback riding tours lead by expert guides who are familiar with the paths and can provide relevant information about the surroundings.
Wear comfortable clothing and closed-toe shoes that are appropriate for riding, and don't forget a cap and sunscreen for sun protection.

How to Get There
Booking: Plan ahead of time by researching and booking horseback riding trips, confirming the meeting location and logistics.

A horseback ride through Puglia's olive fields and countryside is a lyrical adventure that balances your connection with nature and your equestrian partner. As you ride along gorgeous paths, taking in the sights, sounds, and smells of nature, you'll create memories that combine the excitement of adventure with the serenity of the terrain. This unique perspective adds a magical touch to your Puglian experience, encouraging you to embrace the area's beauty in a whole new way.

Outdoor Recreation

Introduction: Puglia's stunning landscapes provide a playground for outdoor enthusiasts seeking excitement, relaxation, and close contact with nature. This section introduces you to the wealth of outdoor activities available in Puglia. Puglia's varied environment provides incredible activities for anybody looking to connect with nature, from breathtaking treks and seaside excursions to water sports and countryside cycling. As you begin your outdoor adventures in this enthralling region, you will discover a world of adventure, tranquillity, and discovery.

6.1 Puglian Beaches

6.1.1 Beaches on the Salento Peninsula

The Salento Peninsula is a seaside sanctuary noted for its clean beaches and idyllic scenery, enveloped by the turquoise seas of the Ionian and Adriatic Seas. Each beach has its own personality and charm, giving sunbathers and nature lovers a variety of options. In this section, we'll go over the best beaches on the Salento Peninsula to help you make the most of your coastal exploration.

1. Prosciutto Punta
Location: Near Porto Cesareo on the Ionian shore.
Highlights: Enjoy swimming and relaxation in crystal-clear waters and smooth, powdery sands.
Arrive early to secure a decent place, and pack essentials such as shade and sunscreen.

2. Torre Lapillo says
The location is near Punta Prosciutto.
Highlights include a family-friendly beach with shallow seas ideal for children. Provides sunbed rentals as well as a variety of seaside facilities.
Participate in activities such as snorkeling, windsurfing, or beach volleyball.

3. Porto Selvaggio, Italy
The hotel is located within the Porto Selvaggio Natural Park.
Highlights: A pristine refuge with rocky coves and sandy expanses. A wildlife and hiking enthusiast's dream.
Pack a picnic and hiking shoes because a route leads to panoramic views.

4. The Bay of Turchi
Location: Along the Adriatic coast, near Otranto.
Highlights: A hidden treasure with shallow waters and beautiful sand. In the middle of olive trees, it provides a sense of isolation.
Exploration: Walk down the coast to locate more

beautiful coves.

5. "Maldives of Salento" Pescoluse
The "Maldives of Salento," located near Torre Vado. Highlights include crystal-clear oceans and exquisite white sand beaches evocative of tropical paradises. Evening Charm: Come in the evening for a peaceful atmosphere and spectacular sunset views.

6. Torre dell'Orso (Orso Tower)
Location: Near Melendugno on the Adriatic shore.
Highlights: A stunning natural beauty is provided by the combination of sandy coasts and limestone cliffs. The iconic "Two Sisters" rock formations should not be missed.
With its shallow seas and beach facilities, it is ideal for youngsters.

7. The Suina Point
Location: Near the coast of Gallipoli.
Highlights: A tranquil haven with clear seas and rocky inlets ideal for snorkeling and exploration.
Nature Walks: For a change of scenery, take a walk among the neighboring dunes and pine forests.

With their breathtaking scenery and welcoming waves, the beaches of the Salento Peninsula are a tribute to nature's artistry. Whether you are looking for relaxation, adventure, or a combination of the two, the Salento beaches have a variety of options to satisfy your coastal appetites. Dive into the azure waves, soak up the rays, and immerse yourself in the magnificence that defines Puglia's coastline.

6.1.2 Beaches on the Gargano Peninsula

The Gargano Peninsula, nestled within the Adriatic Sea's embrace, invites with its variegated shoreline, embellished with sandy stretches and secret coves. This section showcases the Gargano Peninsula's lovely beaches, which offer a blend of natural beauty, recreational options, and picturesque vistas to satisfy every beachgoer's desire.

1. The Zagare Bay
Location: Known as the "Bay of the Gypsies," it is located near Mattinata.
Highlights include a picturesque harbor surrounded by limestone cliffs, sparkling waves, and the iconic sea arch known as "Pizzomunno."
Boat Tours: Take a boat trip to get a new perspective on the bay's splendor.

2. Beaches in Vieste
Location: Along the coast of Vieste, a lovely Gargano town.
Highlights: Choose from a variety of beaches, ranging from sandy beaches to rocky inlets. Scenic beauty meets the convenience of a bustling town.
Activities include water sports, beach activities, and a tour of Vieste's medieval streets.

3. Beach in Cala Puglia
Location: Near Peschici, surrounded by lush greenery.
A private sanctuary with turquoise seas and white sands. It is only accessible by boat or on a wildlife hike.
Nature Trail: For a delightful experience, embark on the magnificent hike from Baia San Nicola to Cala Puglia.

4. Beach of Vignanotica
Secluded along the eastern shore of Gargano.
Highlights: Surrounded by stunning rocks, this beach offers peace and beauty. Its unspoiled charm is enhanced by its limited conveniences.
Climb the cliffs for panoramic views of the turquoise ocean.

5. Beach at Manaccora
Location: South of Vieste, near Peschici.
Highlights include a family-friendly beach with clear, shallow surf and beautiful sands. Provides conveniences for a relaxing beach day.
Relaxation: Unwind in a tranquil setting while taking in the gorgeous scenery.

6. Beaches in Rodi Garganico
Location: Visit the beaches around Rodi Garganico.
Highlights: Explore a combination of sandy beaches

and rocky landscapes for a variety of coastal experiences.
Local Flavor: Visit the town's shore for fresh seafood.

7. Beaches in Mattinata
Location: Enjoy the beaches that surround the village of Mattinata.
Highlights: Relax on peaceful sandy beaches surrounded by dramatic cliffs. Ideal for a day of relaxation and sunbathing.
Exploration: For a nature-filled holiday, visit the Gargano National Park.

The beaches of the Gargano Peninsula are a tribute to the region's natural variability, providing a variety of coastal experiences that mirror the region's various landscapes. The Gargano shoreline has something for everyone, whether you're looking for tranquil coves, lively town beaches, or secluded retreats. Embrace the splendor of the Adriatic by exploring its enchanting beaches and basking in the beauty that marks this coastal sanctuary.

6.1.3 Beaches on the Ionian Coast

The Ionian Coast of Puglia is a paradise of sun-drenched beaches and crystalline waters, providing a tranquil respite for beachgoers and nature lovers both. The beauty of the Ionian Coast's beaches will be shown in this section, where golden sands meet the gentle embrace of the Ionian Sea, promising memorable moments of rest and amazement.

1. Beaches at Porto Cesareo
Explore the coastline around Porto Cesareo.
Highlights: Explore a variety of beaches, each with its own distinct personality. It is ideal for families due to its clear waters and warm shallows.
Boat Tours: Consider going on a boat tour to explore the protected maritime area.

2. The Suina Point
Location: Along the Ionian coast near Gallipoli.
Highlights: Relax on this calm beach with pristine waves and rocky inlets ideal for snorkeling.
Nature Walks: Take a pleasant stroll through the nearby pine forests and dunes.

3. Torre Lapillo says
On the Ionian coast, near Punta Prosciutto.
Highlights: Take advantage of the shallow, tranquil waters, which make it ideal for families. Take part in watersports or simply relax and enjoy the sun.
Local Flavor: Savor fresh seafood at local seaside restaurants.

4. Ugento Marina
Location: Visit the beaches around Ugento.
Highlights: A white-sand haven with blue oceans. It

provides an ideal backdrop for relaxation and beachside picnics.

Historical Exploration: Add a bit of culture to your beach day by visiting local ancient ruins.

5. Prosciutto Punta
The location is to the south of Porto Cesareo.

Highlights: Take in the dramatic contrast between the beautiful blue oceans and the pristine white dunes. A must-see for beachgoers.

Beachfront Dining: Have lunch on the beach with a view.

6. Maruggio Campomarino
Location: A tranquil refuge close to Maruggio.

Highlights include a large stretch of beach with mild waves that is ideal for swimming and relaxing.

Interact with residents who frequent this tranquil beach location.

7. Santa Maria di Leuca, Italy
The southernmost point of Puglia.

Highlights: Enjoy the rocky shores and welcoming seas at the meeting point of the Ionian and Adriatic Seas.

Exploration of Lighthouses: Visit the magnificent Santa Maria di Leuca lighthouse for panoramic views.

The beaches of the Ionian Coast are a haven of

tranquility and natural beauty, where the artistry of sunsets meets the tranquility of crystal-clear waters. Whether you're looking for family-friendly beaches, secret coves, or the adrenaline rush of water sports, the Ionian beaches of Puglia have it all. Dip your toes in the calm waves, soak up the Mediterranean sun, and revel in the tranquil beauty that typifies this coastal retreat.

6.2 Nature and Hiking Trails

6.2.1 Gargano National Park

Puglia's natural beauty extends beyond its beaches, beckoning travelers to explore its different landscapes via hiking and nature paths. In this section, we begin our journey to the Gargano National Park, a biodiversity hotspot with stunning views that promises an immersive experience for nature enthusiasts and hikers alike.

1. Cliffs and forests
Gargano National Park's verdant forests, limestone cliffs, and panoramic views provide an awe-inspiring setting for your hikes.
Hiking paths: Select from a number of paths, each catering to a particular skill level and affording various views of the park's grandeur.

2. The Umbra Forest

Wander through the Umbra Forest, a refuge of old beech and oak trees that creates a calm, shaded oasis.

Wildlife Encounters: Keep a look out for various bird species and wildlife that live in the forest.

3. Trails in Monte Sant'Angelo

Hike the spiritual road to Monte Sant'Angelo, where you'll find an ancient sanctuary and a stunning panoramic view.

Historical Importance: Learn about the historical layers that enhance the hiking experience.

4. Coastal Routes

Spectacular Views: Follow the coastal roads that give breathtaking views of the Adriatic Sea, revealing hidden coves and unspoiled beaches.

Vieste to Pugnochiuso: For an unforgettable coastline excursion, choose the Vieste to Pugnochiuso path.

5. Hiking to Baia delle Zagare

Hike to Baia delle Zagare for a magnificent view of the sea arch "Pizzomunno" and the turquoise waters of the bay.

Rewarding Effort: The trail's reward is an unrivaled beach, ideal for a refreshing dip.

6. Coastal Protected Areas:
Hike to seaside sanctuaries like San Matteo and Santa Maria di Leuca for a mix of natural and spiritual experiences.
Panoramic Views: As you ascend to these lofty getaways, you will be treated to breathtaking views.

7. Planning and security:
Check trail conditions and weather forecasts, and bring essentials such as water, snacks, and a map.
Guided trips: Consider joining one of the many guided hiking trips lead by experts who can enhance your experience with insights and safety.

The Gargano National Park is a hiking and nature lover's paradise, with each track revealing a different aspect of Puglia's environment. This park offers a symphony of natural beauties waiting to be found, from old forests to spectacular cliffs. Lace up your hiking boots, take a deep breath of fresh air, and embark on a tour into Puglia's wild heart to discover the limitless beauty that exists within its natural surroundings.

6.2.2 Salento Coastal Trail

The Salento Coastal Trail encourages you to experience the splendor of Puglia's southernmost region on a scenic trek along its coastline. In this episode, we begin an enthralling journey of the

Salento Coastal Trail, where rocky cliffs, turquoise waters, and historical landmarks weave together to produce a tapestry of natural and cultural grandeur.

1. Visiting the Adriatic Coast:
The Salento Coastal Trail meanders along the Adriatic coast, providing beautiful views of the water and steep rocks.
Discover antique watchtowers and historical sites that bear witness to Salento's illustrious past.

2. Sant'Andrea to Torre dell'Orso:
Coastal Magic: Begin your journey at Torre dell'Orso, a beautiful beach famed for its unique rock formation.
Panoramic Trails: Follow scenic routes that lead to the charming Sant'Andrea, offering breathtaking coastal views.

3. Santa Cesarea Terme to Porto Badisco:
Hike from Porto Badisco, noted for its crystal-clear waters and mystical links, to discover hidden delights.
Natural Baths: Travel to Santa Cesarea Terme, a town known for its hot springs and beautiful architecture.

4. Tricase Porto to Castro:
Coastal Attractions: Explore Castro's medieval heart and limestone cliffs overlooking the sea.

Reach Tricase Porto, a fishing town surrounded by cliffs and a tranquil port.

5. Between Otranto and Santa Maria di Leuca:
Endless Beauty: Finish your journey along the breathtaking Otranto-Santa Maria di Leuca section.
Adriatic and Ionian Seas: Witness the merging of the Adriatic and Ionian Seas at Santa Maria di Leuca, a serene experience.

6. Local Delights and Traditions:
Culinary Experiences: Stop in picturesque seaside towns to sample Salento's culinary treasures, which range from fresh seafood to local wines.
Cultural Encounters: Immerse yourself in Salento's rich tapestry, meeting the kind people along the route.

7. Practical Advice:
Wear suitable hiking shoes, bring sunscreen, and bring drink to remain hydrated.
The Salento Coastal Trail has a variety of terrains, so be prepared for both easy walks and moderate excursions.

The Salento Coastal Trail enables you to see the union of land and sea, where nature's beauty and cultural history coexist along the enchanting coastline. Traverse rugged cliffs, discover hidden coves, and revel in the tranquility that typifies this coastal journey. Allow the sea breeze to whisper tales of a region where history, nature, and the human soul coexist in a peaceful embrace as you stroll the Salento Coastal Trail.

6.2.3 Umbra Foresta

The Foresta Umbra, nestled within the Gargano National Park, calls with its old woods charm and calm beauty. In this section, we explore the enthralling world of Foresta Umbra, a virgin forest that offers an immersive trip through towering trees, colourful flora, and a sense of wonder found only in nature's heart.

1. Ancient Woodland Refuge:
Foresta Umbra, which translates as "Shady Forest," is a monument to nature's durability and ageless beauty.
Flora Diverse: Discover a diverse range of plant species, from towering beech trees to fragile wildflowers, producing a vibrant tapestry.

2. Hiking Routes and Trails:
Tranquil Paths: Hike through the woodland on a network of well-marked routes that cater to walkers of all abilities.
Highlights of the trail include secret springs, panoramic views, and encounters with woodland inhabitants.

3. Path to Monte Sant'Angelo:

Spiritual Journey: Set off on the pilgrimage path to Monte Sant'Angelo, which passes through Foresta Umbra.

Discover ancient monastery sites and immerse yourself in the spiritual aura of the surroundings.

4. Wildlife and Fauna:

Avian Symphony: Foresta Umbra is a birdwatcher's paradise, with opportunities to see a wide range of bird species.

Wildlife Encounters: Look for foxes, wild boars, and other woodland critters that live in the forest.

5. Clearings and scenic views:

Panoramic Overlooks: Make your way to viewpoints that offer panoramic views of the Gargano Peninsula and the Adriatic Sea.

Picnic Areas: Look for peaceful clearings where you can stop for a picnic in the middle of nature's embrace.

6. Sensory Experimentation:

Nature's Music: Listen to the music of rustling leaves, bird calls, and the calm murmur of streams.

Natural Fragrance: Inhale the earthy scents of the forest for a sensory experience that will revitalize your mind.

7. Practical Advice:

Wear comfortable hiking clothes and sturdy shoes appropriate for forest treks.

Guided Tours: Consider attending guided forest tours lead by experts who may give information about the ecosystem of the forest.

Finally, Foresta Umbra invites you to reconnect with nature's rhythm and serenity. You'll be transported in a world undisturbed by time as you explore its quiet trails and beautiful vegetation. Allow the Foresta Umbra to awaken your senses, inspire your soul, and leave you with a deep appreciation for the subtle beauty that lies at the core of this ancient woodland refuge.

6.3 Water Activities

6.3.1 Snorkeling and Scuba Diving

Puglia's coastal wonders extend beneath the waves, inviting water enthusiasts to explore a teeming world of marine life and submerged landscapes. This section delves into the thrilling worlds of scuba diving and snorkeling, revealing the secrets of Puglia's underwater treasures and demonstrating the ideal places to start on these aquatic experiences.

1. Dive Into Underwater Worlds:
Underwater: Puglia's clean waters contain a rich

assortment of marine life, shipwrecks, and underwater structures just waiting to be discovered.

Scuba Diving and Snorkeling: Whether you're an experienced diver or a first-time snorkeler, Puglia has something for everyone.

2. Excursions for Scuba Diving:
Explore the underwater habitats surrounding the Gargano Peninsula, including dive spots displaying vivid coral reefs and marine animals.
Exploration of Shipwrecks: Dive into history by examining shipwrecks such as the "Relitto di San Domenico" near Vieste, an intriguing place for advanced divers.

3. Adventures in Snorkeling:
Crystal Clear seas of Salento: Snorkel in the turquoise seas off the Salento coast, where small coves and secret grottoes reveal marine wonders.

Torre dell'Orso caverns: Explore the underwater caverns near Torre dell'Orso, an ideal snorkeling location with colorful fish and underwater formations.

4. Best Dive Sites:
Dive the Tremiti Islands, a marine reserve famed for its crystal-clear waters and varied marine life.
Cala del Citro: Dive into the underwater

passageways and rich fish life of Cala del Citro for an exciting diving experience.

5. Snorkeling Treasures:
Porto Selvaggio: Snorkel in the pristine waters of Porto Selvaggio, where marine life abounds among the rocky cliffs.
Baia dei Turchi: Snorkel in the shallow, turquoise waters of Baia dei Turchi, which reveal a fascinating undersea environment.

6. Dive Shops and Tours:
Expert Direction: Participate in guided dive trips conducted by qualified professionals who know the best dive sites and assure your safety.
Dive facilities offer introductory classes for beginners, making the underwater experience accessible to individuals who are new to it.

7. Conservation and safety:
Respect aquatic Life: Dive and snorkel responsibly by avoiding contact with coral and aquatic organisms.
Environmental Protection: Contribute to local conservation initiatives to save Puglia's marine environment for future generations.

Finally, Puglia's underwater realm invites you to embark on an adventure that combines exploration with aquatic secrets. Puglia's waters offer a sensory trip filled with amazement and wonder, whether you want to dive deep into the ocean depths or snorkel near the coast. Allow the underwater beauty of Puglia to grab your heart and imagination as you immerse yourself in a world of bright hues, fascinating marine life, and submerged treasures.

6.3.2 Kayaking and sailing

Introduction: Puglia's azure seas and picturesque shoreline are ideal for aquatic exploration. We set sail and paddle our way through the magical world of sailing and kayaking in this section, allowing you to experience the tranquillity of the sea while discovering the hidden gems that Puglia's coastline has to offer.

1. Adventures at Sea:
Sail on the Adriatic or Ionian Seas, where calm winds carry you along the coast, revealing breathtaking landscapes and quiet bays.

Puglia provides a variety of boating alternatives, from classic sailing boats to sophisticated yachts, to suit your sailing style.

2. Routes for Coastal Sailing:
Sail down the Adriatic coast, stopping in picturesque towns like Polignano a Mare and Monopoli.
Ionian Coast: Travel down the Ionian coast, stopping

in charming towns like Gallipoli and Santa Maria di Leuca.

3. Kayaking Adventures:
Glide through the calm seas on a kayak, immersing yourself in the splendor of Puglia's coastline at your own pace.
Coves and Grottoes: Explore secret coves, sea caves, and rocky inlets only accessible by kayak.

4. Kayaking Paths:
Torre Guaceto Nature Reserve: Paddle through the clean waters of Torre Guaceto Nature Reserve, a home for marine life and birds.
Cala dell'Acquaviva: Paddle to the beautiful Cala dell'Acquaviva, a hidden bay accessible only by kayak.

5. Sailing at Sunset:
Golden Hours: Enjoy the wonder of Puglia's sunsets from the deck of a sailing boat as the sky transforms into a colorful canvas.
Set the mood for a romantic evening soaking in the glory of the setting sun on the open sea.

6. Rentals and guided tours:
Expert Direction: Join guided sailing experiences conducted by expert captains who share their local knowledge.
Independent Exploration: Rent kayaks or sailboats

for self-guided adventures that allow you to navigate the shoreline according to your preferences.

7. Navigation and safety
When organizing your sailing or kayaking expedition, keep in mind weather conditions and tides.
Before you go out on the lake, be sure you have the proper safety equipment, including life jackets.

Sailing and kayaking provide a new perspective of Puglia's coastal splendor, allowing you to enjoy the tranquility of the water while discovering hidden treasures along the route. Puglia's seas promise incredible moments of connection with nature's splendor, whether you're sailing under the sun's warm embrace or kayaking into the heart of a sea cave. Set your course, whether by sail or paddle, and let the coastal breeze guide you through a marine adventure that embodies Puglia's seaside charm.

Excursions and day trips

7.1 The Castle of Monte

Castel del Monte is a UNESCO World Heritage monument that captivates visitors with its distinctive octagonal shape, historical significance, and enigmatic purpose. This medieval fortress in Apulia offers a fascinating peek into the past and invites you to explore its secrets.

How to Get There
Castel del Monte is located in Apulia, near the town of Andria. You can get there by automobile, public transit, or guided tours, depending on your starting place.

Frederick II: History and Architecture Built in the 13th century by Holy Roman Emperor Frederick II, Castel del Monte is a tribute to his architectural prowess and cultural legacy.

Octagonal Shape: The castle's most notable feature is its octagonal shape, which is unusual for medieval strongholds. A similar layout of rooms can be found on each side of the octagon.

Symbolism pervades the castle's design, with possible parallels to Frederick II's interests in science, mathematics, and the universe.

Courtyard: Begin your journey in the central courtyard, where the octagonal design is most visible. Consider the symmetry and architectural elements.

inner chambers: Explore the inner chambers of the castle, each with its unique purpose and design. The layout shows that spaces have been carefully divided.

Climb the castle's turrets for panoramic views of the surrounding environment, including the Apulian countryside and the sea.

Goal Debate: Interpreting the Enigma Historians disagree over what the objective of Castel del Monte was. Some hypotheses claim it was a hunting lodge, while others claim it fulfilled astronomical or symbolic reasons.

Guided Tours are the best way to experience and explore: Join guided tours of Castel del Monte to learn about its history, design, and the mystery surrounding it.

Informational Displays: The interior of the castle contains informational displays that provide historical context and thoughts about the castle's function.

Visiting Suggestions
Before you go, double-check the opening hours, admission rates, and availability of guided tours.

Wear comfortable shoes designed for walking on uneven terrain.

Castel del Monte is a time machine that invites you to wonder at its unusual design and solve the mystery of its purpose. Stepping inside will transport you to a moment of grandeur and intellect, where history and symbols mingle. A visit to this UNESCO World Heritage Site allows you to witness the legacy of an emperor's ambition as well as the enduring fascination of an architectural wonder.

7.2 Polignano a Mare

Polignano a Mare is a magnificent seaside town positioned abruptly on the cliffs overlooking the Adriatic Sea, famed for its breathtaking vistas, quaint old center, and vibrant cultural life. This charming jewel invites visitors to explore its narrow streets, enjoy its coastline splendor, and learn about its rich history.

Getting There: Polignano a Mare is located in the

region of Apulia and is easily accessible by vehicle or train from Bari or other surrounding towns.

Panoramic Views: Begin your visit by admiring the panoramic views from the cliffs. A stunning setting is created by the azure seas, craggy shoreline, and lovely houses.

Exploring the Town: Historic Center: Stroll through the labyrinthine lanes of the historic center, which is characterised by white-washed buildings embellished with colorful flower pots.

Piazza Vittorio Emanuele II: The central area is a hive of activity, with cafes, stores, and a welcoming atmosphere for people-watching.

Domenico Modugno Statue: Admire the statue of the legendary Italian musician Domenico Modugno, widely known for his hit song "Volare."

Casa D'Amare Museum: Explore the Casa D'Amare Museum, which uses multimedia exhibits to depict the history and culture of Polignano a Mare.

Grotta Palazzese Beach: Descend to Grotta Palazzese Beach for a unique beachfront set within a natural cave.

Beach Clubs: Unwind at beach clubs along the coast,

which provide comfortable loungers, cool drinks, and direct access to the sea.

Seafood Delicacies: Dining and Cuisine: At local trattorias, where fresh catches are transformed into wonderful dishes, savor the town's seafood specialties.

Guided Tours are the best way to experience and explore: Consider taking a guided walking tour to learn about the town's history, culture, and hidden jewels.

Cliff Walks: Enjoy leisurely walks along the cliffside promenades for breathtaking views of the sea and surrounding scenery.

Visiting Suggestions
Parking: If traveling by automobile, explore parking options ahead of time, as parking in the town center can be restricted.

Clothing and sunscreen: If you intend to visit the beach or beach clubs, carry appropriate clothing and sunscreen.

Polignano a Mare is a wonderful combination of natural beauty, cultural wealth, and coastal allure. The town offers an idyllic escape for travellers wanting a taste of Apulia's coastal charm, from its spectacular cliffs to its lovely streets and inviting beaches. Embrace the environment, explore its treasures, and allow Polignano a Mare's distinct personality to immerse you in its timeless embrace.

7.3 Grotte di Castellana

The Grotte di Castellana, an awe-inspiring underground world near Castellana Grotte, provides a mesmerizing journey through spectacular cave formations, ancient geological wonders, and an immersive subterranean environment. This natural wonder entices adventurers to go beneath the surface and discover the earth's secrets.

How to Get There

The Grotte di Castellana is located in Apulia and is easily accessible by automobile or public transit.

Entrance and Tours for Subterranean Splendors: Begin your adventure by entering the visitor center and participating in one of the guided excursions that allow access to the amazing cave network.

The Abyss: Cave Exploration Descend into the magnificent "Abyss," a large chamber that opens out to reveal towering stalactites and stalagmites that appear to stretch for the heavens.

The White Cave: Explore the "White Cave," where exquisite calcite shapes create a fairytale-like ambiance.

The Grave: Take a look at "The Grave," a hauntingly beautiful cave with gorgeous formations that resemble shrouds and curtains.

The Cavern of Precious Stones: Marvel at the hypnotic "Cavern of Precious Stones," which is covered with sparkling crystals that sparkle like gems.

Expert Guides: Tours are given by knowledgeable guides who provide insights into the caverns' geological history, formations, and the unique processes that produced this subterranean wonderland.

Tour options: Select from a variety of tour options based on your interests and physical abilities. Some tours go further into the cave system.

Advance scheduling: Due to the popularity of the Grotte di Castellana, consider scheduling your tour in advance to reserve your spot.

Wear durable and comfy shoes designed for walking on uneven terrain.

Visiting Suggestions
Temperature: Because the caves are largely stable in temperature, pack a light jacket or sweater, especially if going during the cooler months.

Bring your camera to capture the stunning structures and one-of-a-kind beauty of the caverns.

The Grotte di Castellana is a journey into the center of the Earth, an investigation of geological wonders shaped over millennia. As you walk through the caves, you'll see nature's incredible beauty displayed via fascinating formations that test your imagination. This underground adventure is a monument to our planet's hidden mysteries, inviting you to discover the wonders that lie beneath the surface and contemplate the forces that have formed this incredible underground artwork.

7.4 Torre Guaceto Nature Reserve

The Torre Guaceto Nature Reserve, located between Brindisi and Bari, is a pristine habitat that invites nature lovers to explore its different landscapes. This protected area, with its turquoise waters, sandy beaches, and teeming marine life, provides an opportunity to connect with nature in its purest form.

How to Get There

The nature reserve is located along the Adriatic coast and is easily accessible by automobile.

Beaches: Explore the reserve's gorgeous beaches, which are characterised by smooth sands and clean waters. The beaches are home to a wide variety of plants and animals.

Hiking paths: Traverse the hiking paths that weave through the reserve, providing access to varied ecosystems such as dunes, wetlands, and Mediterranean scrub.

Marine Life: Snorkel or dive in the marine area to see the vibrant underwater life, which includes anything from colorful fish to marine vegetation.

Cultural and Historical Importance: Ancient Ruins: Explore the reserve's archaeological site, which includes the remnants of a Roman home.

Guided Tours are the best way to experience and explore: Consider going on guided tours offered by naturalists and experts who can tell you about the reserve's flora, fauna, and cultural significance.

Eco-Friendly Practices: Respect the reserve's protected status by practicing responsible tourism, such as not harming wildlife or leaving any trace of your visit.

Visiting Suggestions

Start your journey at the reserve's tourist center, where you may get information, maps, and guides.

Bring sunscreen, a hat, and sunglasses to protect yourself from the sun's rays, especially if you're going to the beach.

The Torre Guaceto Nature Reserve exemplifies nature's beauty and persistence, providing a look into a coastal paradise where land and sea cohabit together. The reserve offers an opportunity to enjoy the raw beauty of the natural world, whether you're exploring its beaches, trekking its paths, or diving into its aquatic delights. You may help safeguard this beautiful ecosystem and create memories that highlight the interconnection of life on Earth by respecting its protected status and enjoying the tranquillity of its surroundings.

7.5 The City of Trani and Its Cathedral

Trani, a lovely coastal town set along the Adriatic Sea, enchants visitors with its timeless beauty, historical significance, and the magnificence of its stately cathedral. Trani, steeped in maritime history and architectural wonders, encourages visitors to explore its streets, admire its seaside vistas, and immerse themselves in its cultural richness.

How to Get There
Trani can be reached by train, bus, or vehicle from Bari and other adjacent towns.

Coastal Setting: Begin your tour by wandering along the waterfront boardwalk, which gives spectacular views of the sea, fishing boats, and the old harbor.

Historic core: Wander through Trani's historic core, where tiny alleyways, ancient buildings, and attractive parks create a timeless ambience.

Visit Piazza della Repubblica, the town's core, which is surrounded by cafes and the stunning Trani Cathedral.

Trani Cathedral: Architectural Glamour: Discover Trani Cathedral (Cattedrale di San Nicola Pellegrino), a marvel of Romanesque architecture that overlooks the sea. Take in its delicate details, rose window, and magnificent facade.

Interior Gloriousness: Enter the cathedral to marvel at its soaring arches, exquisite sculptures, and atmospheric beauty. The relics of St. Nicholas the Pilgrim are kept in the crypt.

Castle of Trani: Visit the Castle of Trani (Castello

Svevo), a historic castle that commemorates the town's medieval nautical prominence.

Guided Tours are the best way to experience and explore: Consider taking guided tours to learn more about Trani's history, architecture, and local legends.

Sunset Stroll: Discover Trani's enchantment at sunset, when the golden light bathes the town in a wonderful glow.

Visiting Suggestions
Appropriate Attire: If visiting religious locations such as the cathedral, dress appropriately by covering your shoulders and knees.

Local Cuisine: Savor fresh seafood at Trani's waterfront restaurants and learn about the town's marine culinary tradition.

Trani is a treasure along the Adriatic coast because of its history, seaside appeal, and architectural beauty. The town offers a blend of cultural inquiry and beach recreation, from the spectacular Trani Cathedral to the calm harbor. As you walk through its streets, taking in the atmosphere and admiring its architectural treasures, you'll be engulfed in Trani's ageless attractiveness, a town that encapsulates the essence of Apulia's marine tradition and cultural wealth.

Useful Information

Having practical knowledge at your fingertips before you go on your Puglia excursion will tremendously enhance your travel experience. This section contains helpful hints and insights to help you manage hotels, transportation, currency, communication, and other aspects of your trip to this enthralling region.

This practical book prepares you with crucial knowledge to make the most of your Puglia tour, from choosing the proper lodging to understanding local customs. Let's go into the specifics that will enrich your trip and allow you to thoroughly immerse yourself in the beauty of this diverse and culturally rich region.

Keeping Safe

8.1 Health and Safety Recommendations

8.1.1 Emergency Phone Numbers

Introduction: During your Puglia adventure, your safety and well-being are critical. Familiarizing oneself with emergency numbers and safety procedures guarantees that you are prepared for any unanticipated emergencies and can promptly access help if necessary.

Emergency Phone Numbers
Dial 112 for immediate police assistance. This number connects you to emergency services, including police, in the event of a criminal occurrence or an emergency.

Medical Emergencies: In the event of a medical emergency, dial 118 to get emergency medical assistance (ambulance). This number is critical for emergency medical assistance.

Fire Department: Dial 115 in case of a fire. This number connects you to the fire department, which responds to fires and other incidents.

Travel Insurance: Make sure you have comprehensive travel insurance that covers medical emergencies, trip cancellations, and other unexpected situations.

Health Precautions: Before traveling, keep up to date on any health warnings or regulations. Carry all necessary drugs and prescriptions.

Cultural Sensitivity: Learn about local norms and practices to show respect for the locals and avoid misunderstandings.

Learn Basic Italian words: While many people in the tourism business speak English, learning a few basic Italian words can be useful, especially in less touristy locations.

It is critical to prioritize health and safety during your Puglia trip in order to have a worry-free and rewarding time. You can ensure that your trip is not only entertaining but also safe by learning the emergency numbers and taking the appropriate safeguards. Enjoy the beauty of Puglia while knowing that you're well-prepared for any situation.

8.1.2 Medical Services

Introduction: When visiting Puglia, it is critical to know where to go for medical aid in the event of illness or injury. Knowing where medical facilities, clinics, and hospitals are located guarantees that you can get healthcare services promptly and effectively if the need arises.

Local Clinics: Most villages and cities in Puglia have local clinics that provide primary healthcare services, including as minor injuries and diseases.

Hospitals: Hospitals with more extensive medical services for emergencies and serious medical diseases can be found in larger cities such as Bari, Lecce, and Brindisi.

Ambulance Service: In the event of a medical emergency, dial 118 to request an ambulance. Emergency medical services will respond quickly and take you to the proper medical facility.

Pharmacies (Farmacie): Pharmacies are widely available throughout Puglia. To find them, look for the green cross sign. Pharmacies sell over-the-counter medications, offer advice, and fill prescriptions.

Travel Insurance: Before you leave, be sure your travel insurance covers medical expenses and emergency medical evacuation. Having comprehensive coverage might give you peace of mind.

Language Barrier: Communication: While medical professionals in larger cities may speak English, having a basic understanding of medical words or carrying a translation tool is beneficial.

Vaccinations and Health Warnings

Health Warnings: Keep up to date on any health advisories, immunizations, or precautions to take before your trip.

While no one plans for medical emergencies while traveling, being prepared by knowing the locations of medical facilities and understanding emergency procedures can make a significant difference. Puglia's medical services are designed to provide required care, allowing you to focus on enjoying your holiday while knowing you're well-supported in the event of an unexpected health concern.

8.1.3 Precautions for Safety

Exploring Puglia provides wonderful experiences, and putting your safety first enhances your enjoyment of the trip. This section contains important safety considerations that will allow you to completely enjoy the region's beauty, culture, and attractions while minimizing potential risks.

General Safety Recommendations

Keep Up to Date: To ensure polite behavior and obedience to local standards, become familiar with local customs, rules, and regulations.

Personal Belongings: In crowded settings, keep a tight eye on your belongings and consider using anti-theft bags for added security.

Save vital phone numbers, such as those for local emergency services and your embassy or mission.

Transportation Safety: While public transportation is generally safe, be wary of pickpocketing on buses, trains, particularly in busy areas.

Driving: If you rent a car, obey traffic laws and exercise caution on unfamiliar roads.

Natural Environment: Beach Safety: When swimming in the sea, follow lifeguard instructions and be aware of strong currents.

Hiking & Nature paths: Stay on designated paths, bring water, and notify someone of your hiking plans.

Respect Local practices: Dress modestly when

visiting religious sites and follow local practices to show cultural sensitivity.

Language Barriers: While English is widely spoken in tourist regions, learning basic Italian phrases will help you communicate in less popular places.

By taking measures and remaining aware of your surroundings, you may thoroughly immerse yourself in the wonders of Puglia while also ensuring a safe and pleasurable journey. Accept the culture, scenery, and experiences with assurance, knowing that you've prioritized your well-being throughout your investigation of this fascinating area.

8.2 Local Customs and Etiquette

Understanding and respecting local manners and customs when visiting Puglia can enhance your trip and promote positive encounters with the locals. This section provides insights into the social norms, attitudes, and traditions that are central to Puglian culture, allowing you to genuinely connect with the people and customs of the region.

Interaction and greeting

A handshake is customary when meeting someone for the first time. Close friends and family members frequently greet one another with a kiss on both cheeks.

Maintaining eye contact throughout discussions is a sign of respect and engagement.

Dress modestly when visiting religious sites or more conservative areas by covering shoulders and knees.

Dining Etiquette: Proper Table Manners: Follow fundamental table manners when dining with locals, such as using utensils and not putting your elbows on the table.

Tipping is appreciated but not required. If you're pleased with the service, leave a modest tip or round up the cost.

Respecting Traditions: Cultural Sensitivity To demonstrate respect and appreciation for the culture, become acquainted with local traditions, holidays, and rituals.

Respect personal space and avoid loud conversations in calm public spaces.

Language: simple Phrases: Learning a few simple

Italian phrases demonstrates your want to interact and communicate with locals.

By adopting Puglia's local etiquette and customs, you will form more meaningful connections with the people you meet and gain a greater appreciation for the region's cultural richness. Respecting customs, participating in authentic conversations, and adjusting to social conventions all contribute to your immersion in Puglia's way of life and encourage happy encounters during your journey.

8.3 Language Hints and Phrases

Introduction: While many people speak English in Puglia's tourist districts, making an effort to communicate in Italian can enhance your experience and help you connect with locals on a deeper level. This section provides language suggestions and essential phrases to help you connect with others, show respect for the culture, and manage various situations on your journey.

Language Pointers

Politeness: Because Italians cherish courteous language, remember to use "please" (per favore) and "thank you" (grazie) in your contacts.

Gestures: In Italian talks, hand gestures are frequently employed to express meaning. However, they must be used correctly and without making any disrespectful gestures.

Useful Expressions

Good day: Ciao (chow).

Hello and good morning: Buongiorno (jor-no bwohn)

Hello and good afternoon (bwohn poh-meh-ree-djoh).

Hello and good evening: Good luck (say-rah bwoh-nah)

Arrivederci (ah-ree-veh-dehr-chee) means "goodbye."

Yes: S (as shown)

No (noh): No (noh)

Please: Please (pehr fah-voh-reh).

Thank you very much: Grazie (graht-see-eh)

You are most welcome: Prego (pronounced preh-goh)

Please excuse me: Scusi (pronounced scoo-zee)

I'm not sure what you mean: Non capisco (pronounced non kah-pee-skoh)

Do you speak English? : Parla inglese? (een-gleh-zeh pahr-lah?)

How much does this cost? : Quanto costa? (koh-stah kwahn-toh?)

Where...? : Dove...? (doh-veh, eh?)

I require assistance: I require assistance (oh bee-zoh-nyoh dee ah-ee-oo-toh).

Stazione ferroviaria (staht-zee-oh-neh feh-roh-vee-ah-ree-ah): train station

Fermata dell'autobus (fehr-mah-tah del-loh-toh-boos) is a bus stop.

Aeroporto (ah-eh-roh-por-toh): airport

Albergo (ahl-behr-goh) is a type of hotel.

Ristorante (pronounced rees-toh-rahn-teh)

Bagno (bahn-yoh) is the Italian word for bathroom.

Learning a few simple Italian phrases not only improves communication but also demonstrates respect for the local culture. Using these expressions as you travel across Puglia can lead to more authentic conversations, help you make new friends, and make your trip even more pleasurable and fulfilling.

Introduction to Currency and Banking: Understanding the local currency, banking facilities, and payment choices is essential for having a smooth financial experience while traveling around Puglia. This section discusses the currency, ATM availability, credit card usage, and practical recommendations for handling your money while traveling in the region.

The Euro (€) is the currency used. The Euro is Italy's official currency. It is denoted by the sign €.

Banking Services

ATMs (Bancomat): ATMs (Bancomat) are commonly available in towns and cities and allow you to withdraw cash in Euros. Most ATMs accept major credit and debit cards.

Bank Branches: Most communities have local banks where you may exchange cash, obtain financial services, and learn about traveler's checks.

Accepted Credit Cards: Major credit cards such as Visa, MasterCard, and American Express are generally accepted in hotels, restaurants, shops, and other establishments.

Currency Exchange: Banks and Exchange Offices: Banks provide foreign exchange services, although they may charge a fee or offer rates that are not as beneficial as those offered by exchange offices.

Service Charges and Tipping

Tipping is appreciated but not required in Italy. If service charges are not included, it is customary to leave a little tip in restaurants.

Expenses and Budgeting

Expenses on a daily basis: Estimate your daily spending to assist you in budgeting for meals, transportation, activities, and shopping.

Security and safety

Carry cash with caution: To avoid theft, keep a modest amount of cash on hand for little purchases and use a money belt or a secure wallet.

Understanding the currency, banking alternatives, and financial procedures in Puglia allows you to manage your costs effectively and have a stress-free financial experience. You can discover Puglia's offerings while having the ease of fast accessing your funds by being prepared with a mix of cash and cards.

8.5 Tour Operators and Local Itinerary Services in Puglia

Exploring Puglia with the help of knowledgeable tour operators and local itinerary services can enhance your experience by providing insights, ease, and access to hidden gems. This section introduces you to reliable tour companies and local services that build exceptional experiences based on your interests and preferences.

1. Private Tours in Puglia

www.pugliaprivatetours.com is the website for Puglia Private Tours.

Highlights: Provides customized tours of Puglia, including cultural, culinary, and historical excursions. Make your itinerary according to your preferences.

2. Viva Puglia: http://www.vivapuglia.com/

Highlights: Offers guided trips and experiences that showcase Puglia's unique charm, such as culinary workshops and wine tastings.

3. Puglia Tours: http://www.pugliatours.net/

Highlights: Provides a wide range of guided trips and packages, such as coastal adventures, cultural immersions, and countryside explorations.

Viator - A Tripadvisor Company:
www.viator.com/Puglia/d5538-ttd

Highlights: Provides a variety of customized tours and experiences in Puglia, providing options for a wide range of interests and preferences.

The Thinking Traveller:
www.thethinkingtraveller.com/thinkpuglia

Highlights: Specializing in luxury villa rentals and personalized experiences, allowing you to tailor your Puglia trip to your preferences.

Context Travel:
www.contexttravel.com/cities/puglia

Highlights include expert-led culture tours and walks that develop profound relationships with Puglia's history, art, and architecture.

Aria Luxury Apulia's website address is www.arialuxuryapulia.com.

Highlights: Offers private villa stays, gastronomic adventures, and cultural discoveries as part of its premium travel experiences.

www.pugliaparadise.com is the website for Puglia Paradise.

Highlights: Concentrates on luxury house rentals and concierge services to provide an upgraded and personalized experience.

Take Me Puglia's website is www.takemepuglia.com.

Highlights: Provides customized experiences and tours for discovering Puglia's lesser-known wonders.

ten. Puglia by Locals: www.pugliabylocals.com

Highlights: Matches visitors with local specialists for unique experiences ranging from wine sampling to cultural tours.

Finally, with the assistance of these local itinerary services and tour operators, you can immerse yourself in Puglia's culture, history, and natural beauty while benefiting from their experience and personalized approach. These suppliers may assist you in creating an amazing vacation across Puglia's breathtaking landscapes, whether you want a gourmet experience, a cultural immersion, or a luxurious break.

How to Get Around

Understanding the region's transportation alternatives makes it easier to explore the region's diverse landscapes and cultural riches. This section provides information on the many kinds of transportation accessible, such as public transportation, rental automobiles, and organized tours, to assist you in navigating the distances and destinations of Puglia with ease and efficiency.

Whether you're exploring the coastline, visiting historic villages, or taking day trips, knowing Puglia's transportation network allows you to plan a schedule that maximizes your exploration while minimizing any travel-related issues. Let's get into the specifics that will make your trip to Puglia more delightful.

9.1 Transportation by Public

9.1.1 Public Transportation (Buses and Trains)

The public transit system in Puglia provides a cost-effective and efficient means to explore the region's diverse landscapes, historic towns, and cultural sites. This section discusses how to tour Puglia by bus and train, providing you the freedom to travel between cities, towns, and villages without the inconvenience of driving or parking.

Regional Buses: Puglia has a large network of regional buses that connect major cities, towns, and even distant locations. Buses are an economical mode of transportation for both short and long distances.

Fares and Tickets: Tickets can be purchased at bus stops or from the driver. Timetables and routes are conveniently accessible, allowing you to properly organize your excursions.

Trains: The train network in Puglia connects major cities and towns, providing a convenient and scenic method to travel between sites.

Trains travel frequently on major routes, making it easy to visit Puglia's attractions while taking in the scenery.

Train Types: Depending on your travel choices and budget, you can choose between regional, intercity, and high-speed trains.

Public Transportation Suggestions

Check schedules and itineraries ahead of time, especially for longer excursions, to guarantee a smooth travel experience.

While some transportation employees may speak English, having a rudimentary command of Italian terms can be useful.

Ticket Validation: If you're using paper tickets, validate them at the designated machines before boarding buses or trains.

Using Puglia's buses and trains allows you to enjoy the region's beauty without the stress of driving. Public transportation allows you to visit Puglia's distinctive locations while immersing yourself in the stunning landscapes and local culture, thanks to well-connected routes, low rates, and comfortable travel options.

9.1.2 Metro Systems (if available)

Metro systems provide quick and fast urban transportation in specific sections of Puglia, allowing you to visit cities with convenience and accessibility. This section exposes you to the Puglia metro systems, boosting your ability to explore metropolitan sites while decreasing travel time and congestion.

Metro Systems: Bari Metro: The capital of Puglia, Bari, has a sophisticated metro system that connects various parts of the city, including the city center, suburbs, and significant sites.

Taking the Subway

Purchasing tickets at metro stations or using contactless payment methods such as travel cards or smartphone apps is possible.

Metro systems typically operate on set timetables, with frequent service during peak hours.

Advantages of Using Metro Systems

Metros are a quick and dependable mode of transit, especially during peak hours.

City Exploration: Take the metro to get to the city's major attractions, commercial districts, and cultural venues.

Riding the Metro: Know Your Routes: To properly plan your excursions, become acquainted with the metro map and routes.

Pay attention to station signs and comments, which are frequently in both Italian and English.

Metro systems in Puglia offer a streamlined way to explore urban regions, making it easy to navigate about cities, discover local jewels, and visit significant points of interest. Whether you're a tourist or a local, the metro provides a convenient way to enjoy city life while reducing travel stress.

9.2 Car Rental Introduction

Renting a car in Puglia allows you to explore the region's diverse landscapes, attractive villages, and hidden jewels at your leisure. This section walks you through the car rental procedure, providing helpful suggestions and insights to guarantee a safe and happy driving experience.

Renting a vehicle: Rental firms: Puglia is home to a number of respectable vehicle rental firms, both international and local. Hertz, Avis, Europcar, and Sixt are among well-known rental firms.

Renting a Car Provides Flexibility: Having a car allows you to go off the usual route, visit rural locations, and create your own itinerary.

Reach charming villages, countryside wineries, and natural wonders that may be inaccessible by public transit.

Tips for Renting a Car: Plan ahead of time: Pre-book your rental car, especially during peak tourist seasons.

Driver's License: Make sure you have a valid driver's license from your home country and have it with you at all times when driving.

International Driving Permit (IDP): While not usually required, an IDP is recommended as a secondary form of identification in Italy.

Age restrictions: Confirm the minimum age restrictions for hiring an automobile, as they may differ between rental providers.

Insurance: Get extensive coverage to protect yourself from potential accidents or losses.

Because traffic signs and guidance may be in Italian, consider using a GPS device or a smartphone app for navigating.

Road Conditions in Puglia: The road network in Puglia is generally well-maintained, with roads connecting major cities and towns.

Parking: Look for well defined parking places or garages, especially in old towns with narrow streets.

Renting a car in Puglia allows you to explore the region's unique landscapes and cultural attractions on your own terms. Following these suggestions and selecting a trustworthy rental business will allow you to enjoy the comfort and freedom of owning a vehicle while discovering the true spirit of Puglia at your leisure.

9.2.1 Traffic Regulations

Driving in Puglia allows you to explore the region's scenic landscapes and lovely towns at your own speed. It is critical to understand the driving regulations and restrictions that apply on Puglia's roads in order to have a safe and happy driving experience. This section includes information on important driving legislation that you should be aware of before getting behind the wheel.

Driving Guidelines

Speed restrictions: Stick to established speed restrictions in kilometers per hour (km/h). The speed limit varies depending on the type of road and locality.

Seatbelts: Seatbelts are necessary for all passengers, including the driver, in the vehicle.

Mobile Phones: Unless you have a hands-free system, it is illegal to use a mobile phone while driving.

Children: Children under the age of 12 or less than 150 cm tall must utilize a child restraint system.

Drunk Driving: Drunk driving is strictly prohibited in Italy. Because the legal blood alcohol concentration (BAC) level is so low, it's advised to avoid alcohol while driving.

Vehicles approaching a circle have the right of way. At crosswalks, be cautious and yield to pedestrians.

Parking: Follow all parking signs and regulations. No parking zones are indicated with yellow lines.

Zona a Traffico Limitato (ZTL) Zones: Some historic towns have Zona a Traffico Limitato (ZTL) zones where only approved vehicles are permitted. Avoid these regions unless you have permission.

Documentation

Driver's License: You must have a valid driver's license from your home country, as well as an International Driving Permit (IDP) if necessary.

Insurance: Ensure that your rental automobile is appropriately insured, and keep crucial documentation close at hand.

Emergency Services: In the event of an emergency, phone 112 for urgent assistance.

Local Road Navigation: Road Signs: Take note of road signs and signals, which are typically in Italian. Before you drive, become acquainted with frequent traffic signs.

Roundabouts: Use caution when approaching roundabouts and yield to vehicles already inside the roundabout.

Following traffic laws assures your safety as well as the safety of others on the road. You may easily navigate the region's roads and enjoy the stunning splendor of this enticing destination while promoting a safe and responsible driving experience by understanding and respecting Puglia's driving rules.

9.2.2 Itineraries for Road Trips

A road journey across Puglia is an excellent way to discover the region's varied countryside, beautiful villages, and cultural treasures. This section features road trip itineraries that take you through some of Puglia's most interesting routes, giving a mix of history, nature, and local charm that can only be properly experienced while driving.

1. Highlights of the Adriatic Coast Route: Visit seaside towns such as Bari, Polignano a Mare, Monopoli, and Trani. Admire the stunning sea vistas and clean beaches.

2. The Circuit of the Salento Peninsula: Highlights: Explore the medieval city of Lecce, relax in Otranto, enjoy the gorgeous beaches of Gallipoli, and pay a visit to Santa Maria di Leuca at the extremity of the peninsula.

Highlights of the Valle d'Itria Loop: Explore the famous Trulli of Alberobello, the round town of Locorotondo, and the lovely town of Martina Franca.

Highlights of the Gargano National Park Expedition: Drive along the magnificent Gargano coastline, visit the old village of Vieste, and trek through the

Gargano National Park.

Road Trip Suggestions

Plan ahead of time: Investigate your chosen route, including locations, lodging, and driving distances.

Use GPS or navigation apps to ensure seamless navigation, particularly in rural areas.

Stops: Along the trip, take advantage of local eateries, sights, and cultural places.

Local Flavors: Savor the gastronomic joys of each destination by indulging in traditional cuisine and regional specialties.

Taking a road trip in Puglia allows you to immerse yourself in the region's beauty and diversity while creating lasting experiences. These road trip itineraries offer an unforgettable opportunity to enjoy Puglia's riches at your own pace and according to your tastes, whether you're following the Adriatic coast, visiting the Salento peninsula, meandering through Valle d'Itria, or discovering Gargano National Park.

9.3 Walking and Cycling

Cycling and walking are two immersing ways to explore Puglia's gorgeous scenery, charming villages, and local culture up close and personal. This section digs into the pleasures of cycling and walking in Puglia, offering insights into the region's varied trails, routes, and paths that allow you to explore at your leisure.

Cycling: Countryside Routes: Puglia provides scenic cycling routes through the countryside, vineyards, and olive orchards, allowing you to take in the natural beauty of the region.

Coastal Paths: Ride your bike along the Adriatic or Ionian coasts, taking in the sea wind and stunning sights.

Bike rentals are available in many locations, allowing you to swiftly rent bicycles for your exploration.

Walking: old Towns: Take in the architectural wonders, attractive streets, and local life in old towns like Lecce, Alberobello, and Ostuni.

Nature paths: Explore hiking paths in national parks such as Gargano National Park or along the rough coast.

Guided Walking Tours: Join skilled local guides on guided walking tours to learn about the region's history, culture, and hidden jewels.

Cycling and Walking Safety Tips: Follow marked cycling and walking paths to ensure your safety and reduce dangers.

Wear comfortable walking shoes or bicycle shoes appropriate for the terrain.

Carry water and stay hydrated, especially during the hot months.

Wear a hat and use sunscreen to protect yourself from the sun's rays.

Local Interaction: Engage Locally: Cycling and walking allow you to interact with locals, tour markets, and learn about the culture.

Finally, cycling and walking in Puglia allow you to get up close and personal with the region's beauty, history, and daily life. Cycling through the countryside or wandering along old alleys allow you to discover Puglia's attractions at a slower pace, encouraging memorable experiences and a better understanding of the region's attractiveness.

Travel tips

10.1 Packing Essentials for

Packing for your Puglia adventure necessitates meticulous planning in order to ensure that you have all you need while keeping your luggage reasonable. This section gives you tips on what to pack for your trip, so you can stay comfortable and prepared as you visit Puglia's diverse landscapes, historic cities, and cultural sites.

Pack lightweight and breathable clothing that is appropriate for the Mediterranean environment.

Bring comfortable walking shoes when touring towns, trails, and beaches.

Swimwear: Don't forget to bring swimwear when visiting Puglia's stunning beaches.

Pack sunglasses, a wide-brimmed hat, and sunscreen to protect yourself from the sun.

Adapters: Bring power adapters to charge your gadgets, depending on your home country.

Travel Wallet: A travel wallet keeps your paperwork, passport, money, and cards safe.

Carry a reusable water bottle to stay hydrated while also reducing plastic waste.

Daypack: A tiny backpack is useful for carrying essentials for day travels.

Chargers: Bring chargers for your gadgets and consider bringing a portable charger for backup power.

Download a language app to help you communicate with locals in Italian.

Prescriptions for Health and First Aid: Pack any medications or prescriptions that may be required.

Include simple medical materials such as bandages, antiseptics, and pain medications in your first aid kit.

Miscellaneous: Local Guidebooks: Bring a guidebook with you to better understand the region's history and attractions.

Foldable Reusable Bag: A foldable reusable bag might be useful for carrying items on your explorations.

By packing deliberately and including these essential goods, you'll be well-prepared to enjoy your time in Puglia to the fullest. You may immerse yourself in the region's delights while being comfortable, connected, and ready for any adventure that comes your way with the correct attire, travel equipment, and personal items.

10.2 Photography Tips

The magnificent landscapes, picturesque towns, and vibrant culture of Puglia provide limitless opportunities for stunning photography. This section provides photography suggestions to assist you in making the most of your visual voyage, ensuring that your memories of Puglia are as vivid and engaging as the experiences themselves.

1. Golden Hour Magic: Sunrise and Sunset: For beautifully lit photography, take advantage of the soft, warm light during the golden hours of sunrise and sunset.

2. Photograph Street Scenes: Capture bustling markets, local artists, and ordinary life in towns and villages.

3. Architectural Wonders: old Structures: Capture

the complex features and one-of-a-kind design of Puglia's old structures.

4. Natural Beauty: Coastal Landscapes: Photograph the coast's rough rocks, crystal-clear waves, and breathtaking sea caves.

Capture the rolling hills, olive trees, and vineyards that characterize Puglia's landscape.

5. Culinary Delights: Food and Culture Capture the vibrant colors and textures of Puglia's mouthwatering cuisine.

Cultural Festivals: Document the region's culture by photographing local festivals, dances, and traditional ceremonies.

6. Candid Moments: People: Photograph candid images of locals and fellow travelers engrossed in Puglia's beauty.

7. Textures and Details Close-Ups: For unique shots, pay attention to details such as textures, patterns, and close-ups of local objects.

8. Seek Diverse Points of View:
Low Angles: Experiment with low angles to capture scenes from unexpected angles.

9. Show Respect:
Cultural Sensitivity: Always obtain permission before photographing people, especially in intimate or sacred circumstances.

10. Lens Variety: Bring a lens kit that may be used for a variety of scenes and styles.

Use a tripod or stabilizer to ensure precise images, especially in low light.

Using these photographic tips, you'll be able to capture all of Puglia's beauty. Whether you focus on architecture, landscapes, local life, or gastronomic delights, your images will serve as treasured memories, allowing you to experience the lively essence of this enchanting region.

10.3 Getting Around Puglia's Narrow Streets

The old towns of Puglia are distinguished by their small streets, picturesque lanes, and complicated mazes that beckon you to discover their secret nooks. It needs a combination of patience, adaptability, and a sense of adventure to navigate these beautiful passages. This section provides insights and ideas to help you traverse the tiny streets of Puglia with confidence and ease.

1. Walk: Embrace the unhurried pace of exploring on foot, which allows you to thoroughly absorb the ambiance.

2. Walking with Intention: Keep an eye on your balance because certain streets may be uneven or cobblestoned.

Respect for Space: Be respectful to pedestrians and residents, particularly in tight corridors.

3. Parking and Vehicles: Vehicle entrance is restricted in many historic districts. Park in designated areas and walk about.

4. Navigation and maps: Offline Maps: When traveling in tiny alleys, use offline maps or GPS because signal strength may be limited.

5. Visit During Off-Peak Hours: Less Crowded: Visit historic sites when they are less crowded for a more serene experience.

6. Guided Tours: Local Guides: Consider attending guided walking tours led by locals who are familiar with the area.

7. Capture the Moment: Photography: Use your camera to capture the unique charm of small streets and alleys.

8. Appreciate the Ambience: Cafés and Restaurants: Stop at neighborhood cafés and restaurants to take in the atmosphere.

9. Appreciate the Unexpected: Part of the fun is discovering hidden treasures and unexpected surprises.

10. Be Curious: Allow your curiosity to lead you as you explore the labyrinthine alleyways.

Finally, navigating the narrow streets of Puglia is a delightful journey that immerses you in the region's history and culture. By slowing down, respecting the local environment, and reveling in the charm of these lanes, you'll create unique moments that capture the heart and spirit of Puglia's charming cities.

10.4 Keeping in Touch (SIM Cards, Wi-Fi)

Staying connected when traveling in Puglia allows you to capture and share your experiences, navigate easily, and communicate with loved ones. This section provides information about staying connected via SIM cards and Wi-Fi, allowing you to make the most of your travel without missing a beat.

1. SIM Cards
Purchase: At airports, stores, or kiosks, purchase a local SIM card from a major operator such as TIM, Vodafone, or Wind.

Data Plans: Select a data plan that meets your needs, including internet access and local calls.

Activation: Follow the steps outlined by the supplier to activate your SIM card and data plan.

2. Wi-Fi Hotspots: Many hotels, motels, and bed and breakfasts provide Wi-Fi to their customers.

Cafés and Restaurants: Many restaurants and coffee shops offer free Wi-Fi to customers.

Town Centers and Public areas: Some town centers and public areas provide free Wi-Fi zones.

3. Download Offline Maps: Apps: To travel without using data, download offline maps with apps such as Google Maps.

4. Roaming Fees: Check with Your Service Provider: Be aware of your home mobile provider's foreign roaming charges.

5. Maintain Safety: When utilizing public Wi-Fi, be sure the connection is secure and avoid accessing sensitive data.

6. Emergency Contacts: Emergency Telephone Numbers: In case of an emergency, keep emergency phone numbers and contact information handy.

Staying connected in Puglia improves your trip experience by allowing you to easily explore, share, and document your journey. Staying connected, whether through local SIM cards, Wi-Fi hotspots, or offline maps, allows you to immerse yourself in Puglia's beauty while remaining connected to the digital world.

Finally, embrace Puglia's timeless allure.

As we come to the end of our voyage through the enthralling pages of "Puglia Travel Guide," we hope you've discovered inspiration, guidance, and a glimpse into the enthralling world of Puglia. This guide was created to be your trusted companion, weaving together the rich fabric of this Italian treasure to assist you in creating wonderful moments.

Puglia's amenities are as diverse as they are lovely, ranging from sun-kissed beaches to medieval villages, scrumptious food to exciting festivals. You've begun a voyage that goes beyond the ordinary by exploring its landscapes, tasting its cuisines, and immersing yourself in its culture.

Remember, Puglia is more than a destination; it's an invitation to discover, appreciate, and connect with the soul of Southern Italy. You've become a part of the region's story, whether you're meandering through historic neighborhoods, tasting local wine, or dancing in a traditional event.

Take with you the rich memories, cultural wealth, and friendliness of its people as you wish Puglia farewell. Allow the experiences and insights gathered here to influence your future travels and how you view the world.

May the fascination of Puglia live on in your heart forever, calling you back to complete your trip through this country of boundless beauty and charm. Thank you and goodbye, till we meet again on another voyage.

© **Rick Paul**

Made in the USA
Las Vegas, NV
09 January 2024

84154975R00118